THE MENTAL TOUGHNESS ADVANTAGE

THE MENTAL TOUGHNESS ADVANTAGE

A 5-STEP PROGRAM TO BOOST YOUR RESILIENCE AND REACH YOUR GOALS

DOUGLAS CLYDESDALE COMSTOCK

ROCKRIDGE
PRESS

Cover and Interior Designer: Merideth Harte
Editor: Susan Randol
Production Editor: Andrew Yackira
Illustrations: Imichman/Shutterstock, p. 57; Imichman/Shutterstock, p. 79.
Author photo: Haley Comstock
ISBN: Print 978-1-64152-053-9 | eBook 978-1-64152-054-6

DEDICATION

To my daughters,

Kendall Leigh Comstock
Haley Marie Comstock
Jordin Alyssa Comstock

You are three of the most exceptional people on the planet. I am honored to share this journey with you as your Dad. I love you!

CONTENTS

Introduction **ix**

CHAPTER 1:   **What is Mental Toughness? 1**

CHAPTER 2:   **Step 1: Let Go and Take Charge 13**

CHAPTER 3:   **Step 2: Create a Mission Statement 27**

CHAPTER 4:   **Step 3: Prioritize the Positive 47**

CHAPTER 5:   **Step 4: Flex Your Flexibility 59**

CHAPTER 6:   **Step 5: Step Outside Your Comfort Zone 67**

CHAPTER 7:   **Moving Ahead with Mental Toughness 81**

Resources **93**
References **94**
Index **96**

INTRODUCTION

THE FACT THAT YOU ARE HOLDING A BOOK THAT I HAVE WRITTEN
is amazing to me. Here's why:

In high school, I was in the half of the class that made the top half possible. In college, I didn't do any better. In fact, after maintaining a 1.97 average my first four semesters, I decided to take a year off. That said, when I did return, I maintained a 3.5 average for my final two years and completed my B.S. degree in education. To be specific, physical education. Those who can't teach, teach gym!

My point is this: You do not need to be the smartest kid in the class to make big things happen. In my experience, it is often not the most intelligent person—or the person who has the greatest skill set in a given area—who goes on to be most successful in life. Instead, it's the people who, when times get tough and things get ugly, continually pick themselves up off the ground and keep going. It is the person who has developed, nurtured, and cultivated the highest level of mental toughness who wins in the end. And research backs up my claim: Angela Duckworth, author of *Grit: The Power of Passion and Perseverance*, revealed through her own studies that Ivy League under-graduate students who had more grit (mental toughness) also had higher GPAs than their peers—even when they had lower SAT scores and weren't as "smart."

The broad benefits of mental toughness are huge. You will achieve more, in less time, and with greater ease, regardless of your age. While I can't help you with subjects like algebra, Spanish, or philosophy, I can and will teach you what I have learned on the topic of mental toughness—because I am living proof of its power.

At age 60 I attempted a solo swim of the English Channel, the Mount Everest of open water swimming.

Don't be impressed. I failed.

I swam for 13 hours and 20 minutes, covering 19 nautical miles, two miles short of France. It was at this point, in sight of the shore, that recurring shoulder pain, which I had fought to suppress for over three hours, caused my stroke rate to drop in half. This rate decrease slowed my metabolic rate and caused hypothermia to quickly set in. Knowing that the greatest number of English Channel solo swim deaths occur within a mile or two of shore, my team made the wise decision to terminate my swim.

Despite the fact that I didn't achieve my goal, am I making plans to go back to finish this swim five years later? You bet!

I have also completed the Hawaii Ironman Triathlon more than once and competed in hundreds of marathons, half marathons, half Ironmans, swimruns, Tough Mudders, and too many road races to count. Earlier in my life, in 1990, I had the honor of competing as a heavyweight black belt on the USA Intersport Karate Team in Russia and Poland when Russia was under Communist rule. I have also had several near-death experiences working as an Alaskan *Deadliest Catch*-style fisherman in Prince William Sound, Cook Inlet, and off the Aleutian Islands.

Each of these experiences has taught me a great deal about mental toughness.

Trust me, I'm not sharing my resume to brag or to prove that my brain synapses may not be firing as they should. Rather, I want to let you know that mental toughness can be learned. And my hope is that many of the lessons that have inspired me may inspire and motivate you as well. In fact, I am certain you are mentally tougher than you may even know. My goal is to help you excavate the inner champion you already are, so you can enjoy successes you truly deserve.

In the following chapters, we will talk about how you gain mental toughness through five practical steps. Each step in this program is designed to stretch you and at times can even be a little scary. Throughout the book we will explore mental toughness, drawing on lessons learned through the worlds of the military, sports, business, and, most importantly, mental toughness lessons learned from life.

Each step is meant to be completed at your own pace, so take all the time you need to move through this book. I can't wait to guide you along this journey.

CHAPTER 1
WHAT IS MENTAL TOUGHNESS?

IN THE MOVIE *Rocky Balboa*, the title character, played by Sylvester Stallone, sums up mental toughness by saying, "It ain't about how hard you hit. It's about how hard you can get hit and keep moving forward."

Life can and will figuratively kick you in the teeth. When it does, the choice we are each confronted with is, "Do I give up or do I get up?" Many people, when times are tough, will sit on the sidelines of life, wondering why everyone else seems to have it easy while they struggle to create a meaningful and fulfilling existence. The most important trait that separates those who get up from those who give up is mental toughness. The greatest difference dividing those who consistently achieve goals and those who only set them is mental toughness. I am confident that you can and will create the life you aspire to live by becoming a practitioner of mental toughness.

But in order to begin the journey we have to define what mental toughness is. Mental toughness is the mind-set to boldly advance toward a goal regardless of pain, fear, or circumstance. It is a decision on how you will manage your mind-set, regardless of how much pain you might be experiencing, how fear-filled your situation may appear, and the adverse circumstances you may face along your journey.

Mental toughness is a personal choice. The good news is that you already possess it to varying levels. My goal is to help you excavate it, bring it to the surface so that you act on it, and harness all of the benefits it has to offer.

If you have ever taken on the responsibility of being the primary caregiver to a parent or family member while trying to balance your own life, you are mentally tough. If you have ever planned your own wedding, only to have big changes thrown at you—and you still found a way to keep it together—you already possess a high level of mental toughness. If you have struggled with an addiction or depression and somehow summoned the strength and courage to turn the corner and overcome your disease, you are mentally tough.

One of the most important lessons you'll learn from this book is that mental toughness is not an attribute reserved for a select few. No one in the military, the world of professional sports, or in politics has exclusive rights to it. You may not even be aware of your own mental toughness until you are placed in a situation where you must harness it. Mental toughness can give you the ability to go deep within yourself and then tap into a previously unknown reservoir of courage and bravery.

Qualities of the Mentally Tough

Among other attributes, mentally tough people are flexible, resilient, confident, forward-focused, and determined. They possess the ability to work hard and stick to goals. They are able to forge ahead when most others would quit, and they can prioritize the things truly worth chasing.

I saw each one of those mental toughness traits play out in the life story of a friend of mine. Mike Kittredge was just 16 years old when he started a small business in his parent's basement. He dropped out of college because of a lack of funds. Without a college education, collateral, or life experience, he was laughed out of every lending institution he entered.

Despite setback after setback, Mike's grit and sheer determination allowed him to press on.

Fast-forward 30 years, and Mike has built what we now know as Yankee Candle. At age 47, he sold the company he founded for $570 million.

At its core, Mike's story is not about how one individual can amass wealth beyond the imagination of most. It is not a story about yachts, jets, or mansions. It is a story about the reward of a mentally tough mind-set. It's a story about personal choice and how the mind-set we choose can change our destiny, if not our world.

Here's another example: Anthony Jerome "Spud" Webb, who at 5'7" was one of the shortest players in the history of professional basketball, demonstrated his mental toughness on February 8, 1986. Despite his small stature, Spud Webb won the NBA slam dunk contest, beating his Atlanta Hawks teammate and the 1985 dunk champ, Dominique Wilkins, who stood at 6'8."

Here is the most important thing I want you to know. You have the same mental toughness qualities that Mike and Spud share already within you. The key is to know how to access those qualities at any time and place. You will learn just how to do that through the lessons in this book.

GRIT, RESILIENCE, AND MENTAL TOUGHNESS

Let's try to picture mental toughness as a car manufacturer. Ford, for example, is a brand and under the Ford umbrella are various car models like Focus, Explorer, and Escape. Begin thinking of mental toughness the same way. Mental toughness is the heading (the brand) and the attributes (models) under the heading are words like grit, resilience, determination, guts, stick-to-itiveness, confidence, singularity of focus, hard work, compassion, empathy, patience, never give up, courage, self-discipline, relentlessness, fortitude, and stamina.

Just as Ford has specific models designed to meet the specific wants and needs of each customer, each attribute of mental toughness is used for a specific purpose, designed to achieve a specific goal.

Mentally Tough Benefits

Mental toughness will help you succeed personally and professionally because you'll gain the confidence you need to make positive and impactful improvements in your life. The benefits of developing a mentally tough mind-set are endless because they can be applied to every aspect of your life.

One of the greatest benefits of mental toughness mind-set training is that it will help you manage, if not entirely extinguish, fear.

Why is that important? In my opinion, the biggest obstacle that prevents most people from becoming the highest version of themselves is fear. As you begin to build your mental toughness, you will begin to see fear for what it really is: a threshold over which you must step to become the person you have the capacity to be. How many times have you followed your dream only to find your journey fraught with frustration and failure? Has this fear made you want to quit—or even convinced you to quit? With mental toughness training you will gain the confidence you need to begin crafting a new internal dialogue that gives you the confidence to try instead of giving up.

I am living proof of the value and benefits of mental toughness training. Two weeks after I began writing this book, my wife of 22 years announced she wanted a divorce. My world caved in. At that moment, I wanted to curl up in bed and cry. I was tempted to call my editor and say, "I can't do this right now."

But instead, I took a deep breath and said to myself, "If there ever was a good time to write a book on mental toughness, it is now."

This has been a tough year. My mom died. She was the most positive influence in my life. In addition to my divorce and the grief of losing my mother, my younger sister, Laurie, lived with my wife and me for a few months, while working through her own near-death experience.

I share these setbacks with you because mental toughness training has helped me stay positive and on track while managing the rapidly changing circumstances that now impact many areas of my life. I know the information contained within these pages will help you as it has me.

One of the greatest benefits of mental toughness mind-set training is the ability to reframe your perspective. You will no longer look at the experiences I have described above or similar experiences as catastrophes. You will reframe them as new chapters. A catastrophe can be paralyzing while a new chapter has information to teach. Being a student of mental toughness, you can use the lessons learned in each chapter to help you manage your mind-set and shape your perspective. It's time to experience the benefits you so richly deserve.

Are You Tough Enough?

The first place to begin growing in any new endeavor is to assess your current level of proficiency. I recommend creating a mental toughness wheel to do so. It will help you visualize the components of mental toughness that are important to you, as well as enable you to assess your present level of proficiency for each specific attribute listed on the wheel.

Begin thinking of the outside rim as mental toughness. Mental toughness is a concept more than it is an attribute. For that reason, write the words "mental toughness" several times on the outside rim. On the inside hub (the center of the wheel), write the word "goal" or "target."

On each of the spokes, write the words that you believe most resonate for you about the concept of mental toughness. You might choose words or phrases like grit, resilience, determination, guts, stick-to-itiveness, confidence, singularity of focus, hard work, compassion, empathy, patience, perseverance, courage, self-discipline, relentless, fortitude, or stamina. Use words that you believe will motivate you to be your best self and that resonate with you when you build your wheel. Choose attributes that you presently possess as well as ones you feel will be important for you to develop.

For example, here is a mental toughness wheel that I've filled out:

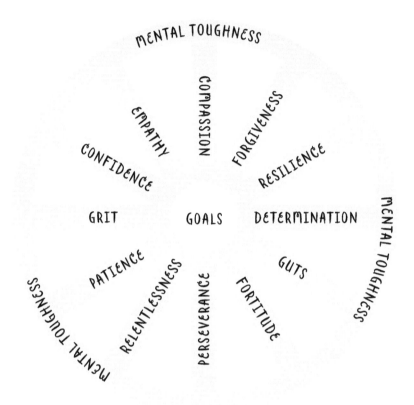

Now, take a turn filling out your wheel:

Once you have your wheel completed, tape it on a wall that you will see every day. Make photocopies and tape them in any area where you spend much of your day, such as the wall of your office, on the top of your laptop, on your bathroom mirror, or the dashboard of your car.

You will also need to look closely at the attributes you have chosen to build your mental toughness wheel. As you begin to examine each word you have selected, take a minute to reflect on what that word means to you. What internal feelings does the word evoke in you? How comfortable and confident are you in using that word to describe yourself? But don't beat yourself up if you feel that a word doesn't describe you well; just note that it is an attribute you want to work on for yourself.

Now, determine your personal proficiency by ranking your capacity for each attribute. Use a scale of 1 to 5, with 1 being the least proficient and 5 being the most proficient. Be honest with yourself—this isn't a test, it's a tool that will help you move forward. Write your ranking for each attribute on the corresponding spoke.

The whole idea is to expand your resources by tapping the strengths you already have and developing additional attributes to carry you even further. Remember, though, that this exercise won't truly be beneficial unless you are completely honest with yourself. You may find that you rank high in some areas and fall below where you would like to be in others. That is completely normal. We're going to work on getting you to a high proficiency on all of these traits as you work through the book.

For the last part of this exercise I want you to think of a person you believe exhibits a 5 for any attribute you have on your wheel. This could be a relative, a teacher (past or present), a neighbor, or a local business owner—anyone who possesses one of the qualities that you associate with mental toughness. Then write that person's name on the corresponding spoke.

You may find that you have inserted the same person's name on many spokes, and that's fine. If you can't think of a specific person for any given spoke, simply leave it blank for now.

One way you can begin cultivating mental toughness is by reaching out to people who are strong in any particular attribute that you have chosen for your wheel. In fact, I want you to reach out to one person whose name you have listed on one of your spokes who has a high level of proficiency for a mental toughness attribute that you want to work on.

Call that person and tell them that you hold them in high regard and value them as the most successful person you can think of when it comes to, for example, grit and determination. Ask them if you could meet with them or speak to them on the phone for no more than 15 minutes to interview them about this subject. Yes, I know making that call will be difficult, but do it anyway! Remember that fear is the threshold over which you must step to become the person you want to be. (We'll talk lots more about moving past fear later in the book.)

Keep in mind that you may get the cold shoulder and never get past the gatekeeper when trying to contact someone you don't know personally. Don't let that stop you. Go to your next spoke, identify another key person, and do it again. I can assure you, if you make enough calls or send enough emails, you will find a person who will speak with you.

Not sure what to say? When you speak with one of your key people you might begin with this statement: "[Insert name], will you help me? I am working hard at developing [insert attribute here] and I cannot think of a person who exemplifies that skill better than you." Here are some questions you can ask during your interview:

» How did you build the skill of [insert attribute here]?

» Did you intentionally set out to build that skill?

» What obstacles did you have to overcome to develop that skill?

» How did you overcome those obstacles?

» How have you used that skill?

» What would you do if you were me to develop [insert attribute here]?

» Who else would you recommend I connect with to develop [insert attribute here]?

» May I call upon you again in the future?

Listen to them. Take notes. Ask them to clarify their answers if you don't understand. Follow up with a thank-you note or postcard that you filled out and stamped even before your meeting (and mail it right away) or send them a thank-you email within 24 hours. This might all sound daunting, but I guarantee that you will be happy that you did it.

Get with the Program: The Steps

Before we move on to the program, here's an overview of the steps that lie ahead.

Step 1: **Let Go and Take Charge.** You will learn to let go of attitudes, attributes, and expectations that hold you back while at the same time moving forward with your strengths.

Step 2: **Create a Mission Statement.** You will craft a mission statement because mentally tough people can easily state their core beliefs, motivations, and personal definition of success. It will help you by defining what you seek to gain.

Step 3: **Prioritize the Positive.** Our words have power and you need to learn how to use that little voice inside your head to express positive beliefs instead of negative thoughts. You will begin to craft and forge a mental toughness track of thinking.

Step 4: **Flex Your Flexibility.** Mentally tough people roll with the punches and recover from setbacks quickly. We will discuss the tips, tricks, secrets, and strategies used by those who have gained this mastery in mental toughness.

Step 5: Step Outside Your Comfort Zone. Learning new behaviors and skillsets is never easy, and developing a new mental toughness mind-set is no different. It won't be simple, but it will be doable. One of the best—and often most difficult—ways to develop mental toughness is to stretch yourself to the point of discomfort. As the Navy SEALs say, "Get comfortable being uncomfortable."

Moving Ahead with Mental Toughness. Mentally tough people don't let their skills slip; they routinely work (even subconsciously) on their toughness, whether through new challenges, reassessments, or in their own unique ways. In this section I will share a plan that contains strategies and tips that you can use to keep yourself on track to achieving any goal, any time, and at any age.

I can't wait to give you the tools and strategies to gain mental toughness. Let's have fun on our journey to a mentally tougher you.

"When I let go of what
I am, I become what
I might be.
    When I let go of what
I have, I receive what
I need."

–Lao Tzu

CHAPTER 2
STEP 1: LET GO AND TAKE CHARGE

THOUGH IT MAY seem counterintuitive, the first step toward developing mental toughness is to simply let go and take charge at the same time. This will require you to identify specific areas that may be holding you back and then let go of those behaviors or traits that no longer serve you. For example, when Nelson Mandela was leaving prison for the first time in 27 years, he said, "As I walked out the door toward the gate that would lead to my freedom, I knew if I didn't leave my bitterness and hatred behind, I'd still be in prison."

What an amazing amount of strength he had to realize that in the moment! This is an ultimate example of letting go and taking charge. With practice, you can also tap into high-quality mental toughness like this.

Letting go does not mean you will immediately extinguish bad habits, behaviors, or thought processes you may have slipped into during the course of your life. Letting go simply means that you will begin to identify, self-accept, and release the things that do not help you advance in the direction of your goals, dreams, and desires. For you, letting go might be the need to release the expectation that conditions need to be perfect before you start a business, run a marathon, or get your PhD. A favorite Marine adage of mine is, "When you're 70 percent ready and have 70 percent consensus, act." That does not mean you should jump haphazardly into the decision-making process. Rather, you need to let go of the notion that conditions must be perfect to take action.

As you move forward in this chapter, you can extract the greatest benefit by journaling your responses in four specific areas:

1. **Pattern identification.** Write down exactly what patterns you believe are holding you back the most. Be careful not to assign blame to anyone, including yourself.

2. **Practice self-acceptance.** Honor the unique gift you are to the world. Write down some of your best qualities (loyal friend, great parent, hard worker, fair boss, and so on). Instead of telling yourself that you are unworthy of life's greatest gifts, practice acknowledging and accepting your worth.

3. **Set your intention.** Write down the traits, behaviors, and processes you believe you should follow to become the person you want to be. Be specific.

4. **Create a letting go ceremony.** Begin by practicing active forgiveness, a mindfulness exercise whereby you give yourself permission to let go of behaviors that no longer serve you. You may do this out loud or by journaling.

Move Beyond the Past by Finding Your Mantra

It is easy to look back on our past and quickly see where we have come up short, underperformed, or even failed. In mental toughness training, it is important to learn from the lessons of our past, while not dwelling on them. In fact, failure can be one of the most important ingredients to achieving massive goals.

The challenge for many people is that they allow failure to become a precursor to their future rather than gleaning the deeper wisdom the lesson has to offer. For many people, a single failure can stop them dead in their tracks. The idea here is to learn from the failure, embrace it, and move on. In mental toughness training, it is vital to embrace your failures for the wisdom they provide.

If you have allowed your past to define your future, it will be important for you to begin crafting what I like to call a mental toughness mind-set. You can begin doing this by repeating the quotes that follow every day. Or, come up with some of your own that resonate for you, and write them down on the lines below. Make sure you say them aloud. Research shows that when we repeat something positive out loud, our brain hears it twice; once through the little voice we each have inside us and once through our ears.

"You always pass failure on your way to success."

—MICKEY ROONEY

*"Success is never final, and failure is never fatal.
It's courage that counts."*

—ANONYMOUS

"It is impossible to live without failing at something, unless you live so cautiously that you might as well not have lived at all, in which case you have failed by default."

—J.K. ROWLING

"Mental toughness is when you find fuel in an empty tank."

—UNKNOWN

"We may encounter many defeats, but we must not be defeated."

—MAYA ANGELOU

*"Strength does not come from physical capacity.
It comes from an indomitable will."*

—MAHATMA GANDHI

Remind yourself that your past does not determine your future. Find a mantra that speaks to you and repeat it, early and often, throughout your day. Write it in the space below.

_____

_____

_____

_____

_____

_____

_____

_____

_____

_____

_____

Take Charge of the Present

Taking charge of the present is important because it requires you to hold yourself 100 percent accountable for everything that happens in your life. Without acquiring the benefits of this lesson, most people will never become the person they have the capacity to be. The lesson is simply this: You must develop the ability to recognize, understand, and honor the difference between a reason and an excuse.

I learned this lesson while working on a fishing boat in Alaska. I was supposed to be ready for my skipper, Jake, to pick me up at 3 a.m. for a three-week boat trip. But when he arrived, I was sleeping off an epic hangover.

After ignoring me for the first few hours of the voyage, Jake pulled me aside and asked, "Why were you late? You knew how important it was to be ready and on time! What happened?"

I tried to come up with a solid reason for my actions. I blurted out, "Jake, I'm sorry. My alarm clock didn't go off!"

He paused for a moment and then calmly said, "The sooner you recognize the difference between a reason and an excuse, the sooner you will take charge of your life and have access to your full potential."

It became crystal clear to me that, up until that point in my life, I had been able to quickly find the excuse in any situation. Acknowledging the reason was another story. Holding yourself accountable is a critical requirement in your mental toughness development because it requires you to take charge of every aspect of your life. It is not always easy to be honest with yourself but when you do, the game changes for you, forever.

The excuse looks for a way to attribute poor outcomes on our part to an event, to a situation, or to someone else. The excuse imprisons our thinking and prevents us from becoming the person we have the capacity to be.

When we hold ourselves accountable—by acknowledging a reason—we begin to look for ways to improve our part in every situation rather than looking for ways to attribute poor performance to extrinsic forces.

Identify Your Excuses

Think about how you may have allowed excuses to creep into your life. Look for ways you may have masked an excuse as a reason and consider how this may be holding you back. Take a piece of paper; write down the excuses you have given recently for problematic situations. Once you have your list, reframe each excuse, this time digging into the real reason behind the problem. As you reread your reasons, what insights emerge? How do you feel? Lastly, identify a solution to step beyond what may be holding you back in each situation. This is mental toughness.

How Excuses Prevent You from Reaching Your True Potential

Often, we create excuses for ourselves that hide the true reason behind what we see as our shortcomings. Although it is understandable to create excuses, in the end they end up hurting us and preventing us from reaching our true potential. Here are few examples: As you can see, in every excuse there may well be an element of truth. However, an excuse doesn't lead to the core of the issue. The key lesson is that when we allow even a fragment of an excuse to justify an outcome, we have lost the chance to grow from that situation. Choosing this road means we will always be looking for the easy way out.

When we hold ourselves 100 percent accountable in any situation, there is a greater likelihood that the situation will have a dramatically different outcome than it would have if we hid under the cover of an excuse. When you are late for an appointment, is it because of traffic or simply because you didn't plan extra time for unexpected delays? When you do poorly on a test, is it because the teacher wasn't fair or because you didn't invest the time needed to study?

Now it's your turn to look inward and honestly assess these situations in your life.

	EXCUSE	REASON	MENTAL TOUGHNESS TECHNIQUE
BUSINESS:	My business isn't doing well because of the economy.	My business isn't doing well because I haven't worked as hard as I need to; nor have I been as creative as I need to be to gain market share.	I will work to correct the mistakes of my past to gain new insights by reading the right books and meeting with others who are doing well. I will work even harder by seeing more qualified prospects and networking with others who can help me.
RELATIONSHIP:	My marriage is a mess because my spouse doesn't care about anything.	My marriage isn't where I would like it to be because I am not doing the work I need to do to demonstrate how important my partner is and how much I value them. I have gotten lazy.	I will work on my relation-ship, independently of what my spouse might do. I will get the help I need to be become a better partner. I will look for opportunities to express kindness, love, and gratitude to my partner because they deserve the best from me. And I will not do this with the expectation of the same in return.
EXERCISE:	I am over-weight because I am big boned, have a slow metabolism, and don't have time to exercise.	I am overweight because I have not made my health and wellness a priority. I tend to overeat, skip exercise, and refuse to maintain habits that will improve my health.	I will begin to make my health a priority. I will figure out the root causes of my overeating. I will reach out to experts who can help me understand why this issue continues to haunt me and I will do the work I need to do to heal from the inside.

	EXCUSE	REASON	MENTAL TOUGHNESS TECHNIQUE
PROCRASTINATION:	I didn't meet the deadline because something unexpected came up and it threw my entire schedule off.	I didn't make the deadline a priority. I waited until the last minute. When my schedule was thrown off, I realized my poor time management would not allow me to finish.	I will start any new project immediately— whether that is a homework assignment, sales quota, or client project—and deliver it ahead of schedule or on time.
LIFE:	My life is unfulfilled. I live in quiet desperation because there is so much negativity in the world.	My life is unfulfilled because I have not done the work I need to do to improve my station in life. I have not worked on my physical, spiritual, and emotional well-being in a long time and it has taken its toll on my entire outlook.	I will begin to make a concerted effort to enhance my life. I realize that if I want to live an inspired life, I must work at it. I will begin building relationships with others who inspire me. I will begin to work out, listen to motivational podcasts, eat the right food, and strive to create the life I want. I refuse to live life as a victim any longer.

Let Go of What You Can't Control

Whether you consider yourself a religious person or not, if you haven't read the Serenity Prayer I recommend you do so. If it gives you tranquility and peace, write it on a scrap of paper or save it on your phone. Leave it within reach where you can reread it or at least be reminded of it at the beginning and end of each day. It is essentially a prayer about letting go of what you cannot control. The best known form is the abbreviated version which reads:

> God, grant me the serenity to accept the things
> I cannot change; courage to change the things
> I can; and wisdom to know the difference.

From an early age, I remember my mom echoing pithy phrases designed to help us reduce, if not eliminate, worry. Phrases like: "Don't sweat the small stuff"; "This too shall pass"; and my personal favorite, "Don't let the bastards get you down."

Each one of the quotes served a purpose. They were my mom's way of telling us to let go of what we couldn't control. A lot of mental toughness training is about learning that lesson so that you will have the energy to take on the things that really do matter. My mother—who had four kids in five years by the time she was 26—understood that life necessitated that she learn essential mental toughness management techniques.

Like my mother did (whether it was consciously or unconsciously), it's important to ask yourself: "What steps can I take right now to regain control and improve my current situation?" Once you identify actionable steps, you will immediately begin to lighten your burden. Here are some sample actionable steps that you can do today:

» Speak to a person who can directly impact the situation.

» Speak to a mentor who can help you put the challenge in perspective.

» Determine a game plan to resolve the issue by creating a manageable and realistic timeline.

» Take a deep breath. There is a good chance that in 24 hours the issue will not seem as big as it does right now.

If there is nothing you can do in the moment to improve your situation, it is simply best to release it, even if only for that day. You can take actionable steps like the ones below to help reduce the angst:

» Get a good night's sleep. It may help you gain new insights and perspective so that you can tackle the issue fresh tomorrow.

» Be kind to yourself. Get a massage or take a long walk; it can help build calm and clarity.

» Break a sweat. There is nothing more effective for clearing the angst from your brain and body than a good workout.

» Call a trusted friend or family member to share your concern. They can often help you gain a new perspective on how you are feeling.

Take action if you can, but also learn to let go of what you can't control.

Act Like You're in Control

Mentally tough people are in control—or at least *act* like they're in control. Recently, I visited a school nurse in Bridgeport, Connecticut. She was the first responder in a medical emergency that required her to deploy an AED (automated external defibrillator) on the parent of a student. The parent survived.

Two hours after the incident, I was at the school, as one of my companies manages and maintains AEDs for clients across the United States. I told the nurse that I was not there to service the device, as that could have waited another day or two. Rather, I was there simply to give her a hug. As I hugged her, tears began to stream down her face. The event now behind her, it was time to allow the pressure valve to release. This often happens once an emergency is resolved.

Even though she had never before been called upon to be the first responder in a life or death situation, she had held it together. She had remained in control—and her control led directly to a life being saved. Talk about mental toughness!

The nurse told me that internally she felt anything but in control. In my opinion, that is the essence of being mentally tough. It is being able to stay on task and in control on the outside, while having the feeling of complete lack of control on the inside.

How was she able to do that?

By simply practicing the skills she might need someday in that specific kind of emergency. She had rehearsed the scenario over and over in her mind, as well as in ongoing training, to reinforce the skill set. Eventually, it had become part of her mental programming.

Here are some ways that you can gain control or act like you are in control:

» Above all else, remember to stay calm. Say those words—"Stay calm"—in your head or out loud if you need to.

» Identify in advance how things might possibly go wrong and think about optimal ways to respond.

» Practice the skills you may need for any situation you think you might encounter.

» Exhibit the attributes someone in that situation would convey, whether it's grit, calm, or something else entirely.

HEALTHY MIND, HEALTHY BODY

One of the most important steps in taking charge of your life is maintaining an active interest in your physical, spiritual, and emotional well-being. Active interest in your life is vital to staying on track in developing your mental toughness. It also helps you let go of the angst from the responsibilities of daily living, boosts the immune system, gives you inspiration, and cleanses the soul.

For many people, maintaining an active interest in their well-being requires a level of effort and commitment they are not prepared to invest in themselves. From there, it is easy to slip into a life of passive interest at best. This can lead to despair, depression, and drama. When Henry David Thoreau wrote the following passage in *Walden*, he may very well have been referring to those passively interested in their lives: "The mass of men lead lives of quiet desperation."

Instead, take charge by letting go. Get rid of bad health habits and take charge by beginning a daily regimen to move your body and strengthen your mind. Movement fertilizes life, so whatever it is that is calling you, take charge by being actively engaged in it. Learn to play the piano, practice yoga, join a book club, take a dance class—you get the idea. As you become more actively engaged in your life, you'll feel the burden of your journey simply exit your body.

You don't need to be in an emergency situation to act like you're in control. When you plan your next step toward your goals and prepare to execute it, consider the skills or attributes you want to convey. Imagine what could go wrong, sift out the issues you cannot change, and practice the most effective mental toughness responses. Again, as you begin working on these techniques they may not feel natural. You may feel that you are only putting on an act. Let that be okay—no skill is built overnight and with time it will become part of who you are.

As you move forward through the book, let the principles of this chapter serve as your foundation and guide. Give yourself permission to forgive the mistakes of your past while letting go of whatever it is that no longer serves you. As you begin to nurture new patterns, processes, and procedures, be persistent, yet patient. The benefits will not come overnight, but with time and effort they will come. It is a new day, a new destiny, and a new you. Focus on these lessons to move forward in the book and in your mental toughness development.

"Without a mission statement, you may get to the top of the ladder and then realize it was leaning against the wrong building."

–Dave Ramsey

CHAPTER 3
STEP 2: CREATE A MISSION STATEMENT

MENTALLY TOUGH PEOPLE can easily state their core beliefs, motivation, and personal definition of success. I know right now it is hard for you to do this if you don't feel mentally strong. And that is perfectly okay. As we work though this chapter you will use the elements provided to discover your goals and create a mission statement that will enable you to stay mentally tough through any and all challenges and setbacks.

The importance of being able to see something that is not present reminds me of my favorite passage in the Bible on faith: "Faith is the substance of things hoped for, the evidence of things not seen." (Hebrews 11:1).

Being able to imagine what you want your future to look like is essential in mental toughness mind-set training. All things are created twice. There is a mental creation first, followed by a physical creation. The order is important because the physical manifestation follows once the mental image has been created. In mental toughness mind-set training, I refer to this idea and practice as pre-playing, or more specifically, pre-playing a positive path to the future. When I refer to pre-playing the future, I mean you need to make a concerted effort to create positive, visual imagery that supports what you would like your future to look like and the goals you intend to achieve. Think of it as a road map that takes you where you want to go in your life.

Many athletes pre-play their future by using visualization techniques to guide them to victory. Consider Lindsey Vonn, arguably one of the most successful skiers in the history of the sport. The gold medal winner attributes much of her success to the competitive advantage she gains by mental practice. Vonn stated, "I always visualize the run before I do it. By the time I get to the start gate, I've run that race 100 times already in my head, picturing how I'll take the turns."

Another one of my favorite examples of pre-playing is from world-renowned comedian and actor Jim Carrey. Like many other young entertainers, Carrey moved to Hollywood at the age of 19 and struggled to find success. In 1985, he drove his old car up into the Hollywood Hills and sat there looking out over Los Angeles, thinking about how despite growing up in poverty in Canada, his parents did all they could to support him. He daydreamed of success. To give himself an achievable goal, he wrote himself a check for $10 million and wrote "acting services rendered" in the memo line. He dated it for Thanksgiving 1995 and kept it in his wallet. The check remained there as something to aspire to.

In 1994, Carrey starred in *Ace Ventura: Pet Detective*, *The Mask*, and *Dumb and Dumber*—an impressive run full of hard but fun work. Just before Thanksgiving 1995, he found out he was going to make $10 million from *Dumb and Dumber* due to the film's wild success in the box office. He soon became the most famous comedic actor at the time. When his father passed away, Carrey slipped the check he had written years before in the casket to be buried with him.

Jim Carrey was able to set achievable goals because he gave himself a way to manifest his success. When we are feeling lost in our life we need to identify our path in order to gain direction. We can't start walking in a direction without knowing where we want to end up. It's also important to remember that the dollar amount on the check wasn't his true motivation; instead, it was to have a life where he didn't have to worry ever again about living in poverty, and to fulfill his dream of being an actor.

One of the best ways for you to implement the techniques discussed here into your life is to develop a personal mission statement. This will keep you on track and serve as your personal road map to success. It reaffirms who you are, puts your goals on target, and moves your ideas into the real world. Your personal mission statement makes you the captain of your own ship by charting a course to the destiny of your dreams. Later in this chapter I will share an exercise to help you begin crafting your own personal mission

THE POWER OF VISUALIZATION

Believing you have already achieved a specific goal by visualizing a positive outcome is one of the most powerful tools you can carry in your mental toughness toolbox. The more detailed your visualization of the sequence of steps necessary to take you to your goal, the more likely you will achieve a successful outcome.

Research in *The Journal of Consulting Psychology* suggests that we can alter the brain by believing and visualizing our success. Immediate benefits of visualization include increased motivation, clarity of vision, increased output of positive thoughts, boost in performance, and reduction of stress.

statement. But before we start on that, there are a few tasks we need to take care of first.

Identify Your Core Beliefs

Think of a core belief as how you see yourself rather than what you aspire to be. Our core beliefs are the foundation upon which we see ourselves, and it is through the lens of those core beliefs that we evaluate other people, the world, and the future. Because our core beliefs are so vital to how we move through the world, it is essential to identify what they are.

If you are one of the fortunate few, your core beliefs are constructive, forward-focused, and positive. However, if you are like many, limiting thoughts may define your core beliefs. If left unchecked they can prevent you from becoming the best possible version of yourself.

Mentally tough people identify their core beliefs and work diligently to convert limiting core beliefs into positive ones where necessary. They then align their life direction in congruence with their new and empowered core beliefs. It is important to make sure that your core beliefs are your own and not a directive given to you by a parent, spouse, society, or other influencer in your life. You can't set goals—something all mentally tough people do—without understanding and acknowledging your core beliefs.

Have you ever thought about what your core beliefs are? If you have, congratulations! If not, don't stress about it. In fact, when I ask coaching clients to write down their core beliefs on a sheet of paper, most get stuck during the exercise and are not sure what their core beliefs are even though they know they have them. Think of your core beliefs as your internal operating system. They subconsciously direct our thoughts, patterns, and behaviors, influencing life in a way that may not always be in our favor.

If you consistently fall short of your goals or live an unfulfilled life in quiet desperation, there is a good chance your core beliefs need adjustment. Consider this: The blueprint created by your core beliefs becomes the master plan for all of your actions and achievements.

It's important to note that your core beliefs are neither good nor bad, they simply are. I want you to embrace that because part of building a mental toughness mind-set is acknowledging and accepting who you are and where you are today as you forge a new future. If you are not where you want to be with respect to your core beliefs, with time and hard work, you will be creating a mentally tough version of yourself. For today, regardless of what your core beliefs may be, don't be too hard on yourself.

Many companies publish a set of core beliefs to give something for employees to aspire to. Yahoo features short one-word values like Excellence, Innovation, Teamwork, and Fun. Starbucks core beliefs are a little more detailed: "Creating a culture of warmth and belonging, where everyone is welcome; Acting with courage, challenging the status quo and finding new ways to grow our company and each other; Being present, connecting with transparency, dignity and respect; Delivering our very best in all we do, holding ourselves accountable for results."

Even though these core beliefs are driven by corporate motivations instead of internal personal ones, the businesses understand they are vital to their overall success. By stating these core beliefs, they are taking ownership over themselves.

I remember the first time I did a core belief exercise. It nearly brought me to my knees. I quickly realized one of my core beliefs was the feeling that I wasn't good enough. Even though my parents did a great job instilling confidence in me and making me feel that I was valued and loved, all it took was a third grade teacher to knock me down. The daily sarcasm and the negative comments she wrote on my quarterly report cards were enough to make me doubt my intellect and question my self-worth. It wasn't until many years later that I was able to identify her as having a major impact on that core belief. I truly believed I wasn't good enough.

It is important to note that when we challenge a limiting core belief and conquer it, we begin to build confidence and courage. Those long-held limiting beliefs simply begin to fade into the recesses of our mind. It is not a question of whether there will be times when you are knocked to your knees because of a limiting core belief; instead, the question becomes, "What will you do about it?" By identifying your core beliefs and knowing how to respond to them in times of stress, you will prevail.

Write Down Your Core Beliefs

If you have not identified your core beliefs and written them down, do it now. Below are a few positive core beliefs; simply check off the ones that you feel belong to you. Add your own to the lines below.

- ○ I am good enough
- ○ I am kind
- ○ I am faithful
- ○ I am compassionate
- ○ I am spiritual
- ○ I am smart
- ○ I am lovable
- ○ I am interesting

List your own in the space below.

_____

_____

_____

_____

Unfortunately, the reality of being a human being with feelings is that some of your common core beliefs are negative in nature. We are going to identify them in order to improve and fix them—we simply do not want to dwell on the negative here. Which of these negative core beliefs do you hold?

○ I am not good enough

○ I am mean

○ I am unreliable

○ I am insensitive

○ I am not spiritual

○ I am dumb

○ I am unlovable

○ I am boring

List your own here in the space provided.

_____

_____

_____

_____

Now really think about these attributes that you have identified in yourself. Embrace the positive ones: You are a good person and have great qualities. Now, let's look at the negatives. Believe it or not, you are going to embrace these too by thinking about how they are not true; or if they are, it's because they are shortsighted assessments of your abilities. The best part of identifying your core beliefs is realizing that they can be modified and changed. If you feel that you are mean, you can take steps to be kind by practicing patience with those around you or volunteering for a local charity. If you feel that you are boring—and chances are good you are not—you can take steps to be interesting by reading about new things or engaging in new experiences.

Identifying your core beliefs (both positive and negative)—and challenging them when necessary—is an important skill you need to develop on your way to mental toughness.

THE SO WHAT METHOD

Our core beliefs often come to us automatically without even thinking about them. When they are triggered, they arrive so quickly that we are often unprepared to handle them constructively, so we automatically revert to the limiting core belief we previously held.

The good news is that with work, we can override our limiting core beliefs and convert them into core beliefs that are powerful and constructive.

One of the best ways to begin changing your inner dialogue is to first identify your limiting core beliefs and then use what I refer to as the "So What Method." This allows you to validate that you have a specific limiting core belief but that you refuse to allow it to define you or hold you back. Use the box below to fill in your triggers and limiting core beliefs, and then get working on converting those thoughts.

The statement "So what?!" is one of the most powerful statements you can use when doubt seeps into your inner dialogue because it almost immediately helps you banish those negative feelings. People who have mental toughness don't dwell on doubt, especially when it comes from the outside world. They have trained themselves to reframe negative thoughts into positive ones by focusing on the core belief they know to be true instead of the assumptions of others.

The reason we need to identify limiting core beliefs and then work at converting them is because these thoughts directly affect our ability to achieve our goals and to become the person we have the capacity to be. Take the time you need to complete this So What exercise to see how your limiting core beliefs may be holding you back.

CORE BELIEF TRIGGER	LIMITING CORE BELIEF	CORE BELIEF CONVERTED THOUGHT
You don't earn enough money.	I am a loser.	SO *WHAT?!* I've earned my degree and will begin work full time in an industry I love.

MAINTAIN YOUR MORAL COMPASS

Years ago, I was working aboard the Krystal Sea in Alaska. An hour after leaving shore, we were in 40-foot seas. Twice, our 150-foot vessel was plucked from the ocean and thrown back into the sea the way a pro wrestler throws a lesser opponent to the mat. I was petrified! But I noticed how still the ship's compass was. Despite how much the ship was being thrown about, the compass gently swayed in the protective fluid of its housing.

That compass became an important metaphor for life. Just as a ship has a compass, each of us has been blessed with a moral compass. Regardless of how chaotic life can be, your internal compass gently pivots, protected, pointing the way to a fulfilling life. The question is, "Will you listen to it?"

The course many of us have plotted for our life's journey is sometimes a direction contrary to the heading of our moral compass. I am confident the greater the gap between where our moral compass points and the actual direction we have been living our life, the greater the feeling of emptiness.

As you forge ahead in your mental toughness training, you will learn to listen to your moral compass through your core beliefs and do your best to follow it, because your goals are determined by your core beliefs. By following your moral compass, I assure you that you will become the mentally tough person you want to be.

Define Success on Your Own Terms

Mentally tough people chart their own path and determine their own future. They do not follow the expectations of others or allow societal pressures to define their success. In other words, they are not in the people-pleasing business.

A speech coach taught me one of the more important lessons of my speaking career, which also applies to the topic of mental toughness. He said, "Two percent of your audience will not like you. They may not like your message, your voice, or even the color of your tie. Let that be okay! Don't let them define your destiny or determine your success."

Often in life, we become so concerned about pleasing the minority that we allow our lives to be dictated by how those who don't matter define our success. Because of them we become concerned with things like:

- ○ What they think of us
- ○ If they will approve of what we wear, say, or do
- ○ What kind of car we drive
- ○ Where we live
- ○ The size of our home
- ○ What we do for a living
- ○ How much money we earn
- ○ Where our children attend school

Other: _____

Other: _____

Other: _____

Other: _____

If we're not careful, others will become the masters of our destiny because we will play right into their version of what our life should be. These others may be people we value, but if our greatest concern is to seek their approval at the expense of being authentic to ourselves, we lose our ability to honor what is best for us.

Mentally tough people chart their own course and define their own destiny. They do not follow the expectations for success others have set for them or allow others to make plans for their future. Throughout our mental toughness training we define success by the ability to follow the calling of our authentic self. It is only by sharing your authentic self that you can truly

IMPRESS YOURSELF, NOT OTHERS

In life, it is tempting to chase things that don't matter. We are bombarded by the lure of advertising and conditioned to believe that more is better. If we are not careful, the barometer by which we measure success will not be defined by what is best for us, but rather how our material possessions measure up to the ones possessed by our neighbors, family, and friends.

Here are five ways to celebrate and honor your unique path:

1. PRACTICE SELF-LOVE: Stop doing the things that hurt you.

2. FOCUS ON CONTENTMENT BEFORE WEALTH: Seek emotional and spiritual ways to fulfill yourself.

3. LIVE WITHIN YOUR MEANS: Don't buy things you can't afford and that will cause you financial woe.

4. OVERCOME FEAR: Do not be afraid of having less. Be content with having only what you need.

5. ENJOY LIFE: Maintain an active interest in your spiritual, physical, and emotional well-being instead of an active interest in material things.

It's time for you to honor the unique gift that you are to the world. Part of that involves impressing yourself, rather than others. Slow down, take a deep breath, and be impressed by how much you continue to grow and give.

become a success and the highest possible version of the person you have the capacity to be. Identify what you need to improve, accept where you are presently while working on a better version of yourself, release, and move on.

In this spirit, write down your true version of success. For some it will mean finding more time to serve others; for others it will mean living a simpler life; for still others it will mean status at work. Whatever success means to you, you need to define it.

Write your definition of success below:

_____

_____

_____

Determine Your Motivation

What motivates you? How can you determine what really gets you fired up? Do you know if you are a self-starter or need extrinsic motivation? In mental toughness training it is important to understand if your previous motivations have been defined by societal expectations or by what your heart is calling you to do. One of the greatest benefits of mental toughness training is to help you identify your life's purpose so at the end of the day when you place your head on your pillow, you will feel good about the person you have chosen to be. And once you identify your motivations, you will find it easier to be mentally tough.

A friend of mine was working countless hours each week in a high-paying, high-stress job. She realized she was being motivated not by what her life calling was but rather by the social pressures she bought into. After years of soul searching, she quit her job and began a full-time career as a Peace Corps volunteer in South America. Even though she was now working for pennies per hour, she found a place of personal peace.

One must be mentally tough to leave a high-paying job for a lower-paying job and jump into the fear of the unknown. Many people will stay in unfulfilling jobs for their entire careers for the sake of playing it safe. Mentally tough people make important life decisions based on what will help them live an authentic life, instead of making their choices based on what they are paid or what others think.

One of the best ways to determine what gets you motivated is to evaluate how you spend your time. I don't just mean what you do with your time but what also occupies your emotional space. My friend spent hours thinking about living a simple life, in service to others, yet felt trapped by the choices she made for her personal journey. By determining what motivates you, you can avoid feeling unfulfilled and find a more enriching life.

For this exercise, ask yourself this simple question: "Why do I do what I do?" In your answer, I want you to use the simple phrase "So that..." For example, you can ask, "Why do I stay at my current job although I'm not very happy?" Maybe your answer is "So that I can provide for my family," or "So that I don't have to make a change."

By using this phrase, you will show yourself your true motivation for why you do what you do. (And you will discover something new about yourself, I promise.)

In the lines below, write down "So that..." statements for each area where you want to determine your motivation.

Why do I _____ ?

So that _____ .

Why do I _____ ?

So that _____ .

Why do I _____ ?

So that _____ .

Now look at your answers. Does it seem like you're doing things in your life for the right reasons—or because it is what you are expected to do?

This exercise should help you gain direction and enthusiasm so you can work on the things that matter to you. Your statements will give you the freedom to choose, act on, and excel in the things that truly motivate you, and help you turn away from the things that you don't care about. This exercise helps you to dig deeper and discover why you do what you do. It will make your quest for mental toughness easier and better.

Set Goals

Developing attainable goals is critical for managing your mental toughness. When you are writing your mission statement, make sure that you are considering what your goals are.

But while setting goals is easy, achieving them can be a very different story. The most important question to ask before setting any goal is "Why?" Specifically, why is this goal vital to me? When there is a clear connection with your why, the how will follow. Your why is the emotional connection or the bond that you form with your goal. Setting goals will also make you mentally tough.

James Cash Penney—better known as the founder of the department store J.C. Penney—has a great quote regarding goals: "Give me a stock clerk with a goal, and I will give you a man who will make history. Give me a man without a goal, and I will give you a stock clerk."

The why happens in the part of our brain that allows us to form an emotional connection with our goal. It is our emotional connection that profoundly increases the likelihood of success. Our emotional connection is formed in a complex set of brain structures located on both sides of the thalamus known as the limbic system. The limbic system serves a variety of functions including epinephrine flow, emotion, behavior, and motivation.

Setting and achieving goals is an important part of succeeding with mental toughness. My favorite tip is to identify your goals and write them down. A *Harvard Business* study found that the 3 percent of graduates from their MBA program who wrote down their goals ended up earning 10 times as much as the other 97 percent put together 10 years after graduation. At first, this is a surprising statistic, but the more you think about it, the more it makes sense. How can you aim for and accomplish your goals without knowing what they are? Do you find yourself working hard but not necessarily knowing what you are working toward?

Setting goals does a number of things that can help you on the journey to becoming mentally tougher. It helps you reduce stress and improve your performance. It gives you a way to measure your growth and provides you with motivation to continue growing. It helps you define what success means to you. It makes imagining success tangible, and this is extremely important in your journey toward mental toughness.

The easiest way to set goals and accomplish them is to use the SMART method. SMART stands for Specific, Measurable, Achievable, Realistic, and Timely.

Writing SMART goals sets you on your way to creating a mission statement that will help you accomplish what you want in the realm of mental toughness. Do you want to run your first 5K marathon? Use SMART goals to set yourself up for success by creating a plan that will help you work toward and reach this goal.

Here's how you would set out to reach the goal of running a 5K marathon with the SMART method:

Specific: I will train until I can run 5K without stopping.

Measurable: I will run 1K for two weeks, then add 1K every two weeks after that until I reach 5K.

Achievable: By building on the distance bit by bit, I can achieve my goal.

Realistic: Breaking the distances down into manageable pieces makes it realistic.

Timely: I will be able to run this distance in 10 weeks.

Write at least three goals in the spaces below with the mission statement in mind. Defining what your goals are will help directly inform what your mission statement is. Take your time with these and explore what really motivates you. This is an important step in your march toward mental toughness.

GOAL:
_____

Specific:
_____

Measurable:

Achievable:

Realistic:

Timely:

GOAL:

Specific:

Measurable:

Achievable:

Realistic:

Timely:

GOAL:

Specific:

Measurable:

Achievable:

Realistic:

Timely:

TOOLS TO HELP YOU ACHIEVE ANY GOAL

These five essential tools can help you achieve any goal, any time, and at any age.

1. **TAP INTO TRIBAL KNOWLEDGE:** Begin networking with people who have achieved exactly what it is that you want to accomplish. They will provide wisdom, inspiration, and a road map for your success.

2. **BECOME AN EXPERT ON THE SUBJECT MATTER:** Read books, watch videos, have conversations. Mastery of the subject matter will propel you forward.

3. **DO THE WORK:** Nobody can do your push-ups for you. Give yourself permission to succeed with relentless pursuit and an unmatched work ethic.

4. **BE PATIENT, BUT PERSISTENT:** Your goals will not come overnight, and you will surely have moments of self-doubt and want to quit. Don't. Instead, be patient but persistent.

5. **BENCHMARK YOUR PROGRESS:** Measure where you are today and compare it to your goal at intervals to determine what adjustments need to be made, if any.

Design Your Mission Statement

Before I speak at a mental toughness event, I do my homework on the company I'm addressing. In addition to conducting research, I make sure to ask for their mission statement in order to gain insight into the corporate culture. I often receive mission statements that are three or four paragraphs long. Unfortunately, these lengthy mission statements are often meaningless, crafted so those in the boardroom can feel good about them. In reality, the message rarely trickles down to the staff. As you start to fashion your own personal mission statement, consider some of the best company mission statements that are short, but to the point.

Patagonia: "Build the best product, cause no unnecessary harm, use business to inspire and implement solutions to the environmental crisis."

Honest Tea: "To create and promote great-tasting, healthy, organic beverages."

Life is Good: "To spread the power of optimism."

LinkedIn: "To connect the world's professionals to make them more productive and successful."

Alibaba: "To make it easy to do business anywhere."

Sony: "To be a company that inspires and fulfills your curiosity."

Amazon: "To be Earth's most customer-centric company; to build a place where people can come to find and discover anything they might want to buy online."

My personal mission statement is short and sweet, yet articulates my life's purpose: "To live my best life by inspiring others to become actively engaged in their physical, spiritual, and emotional well-being."

My mission statement is 19 words long. I recommend creating yours in 40 words or less because anything longer is more than likely not going to be something you can remember or internalize. Reciting your mission statement—to yourself and others—should become second nature to you. So it makes sense that it should be something short enough to memorize, but meaningful enough to have an impact.

When you begin crafting your mission statement, go back over your core beliefs, your personal definition of success, what motivates you, and, most importantly, the goals that you wrote down previously. Keep it clear and concise. You can write it as a statement or as bullet points. How you craft it is less important than what you want to express. Remember, a mission statement is useless unless it's written down, memorized, and completely absorbed. Have fun with this—and most importantly, don't rush it. Take your time and use the lines on the next page to start crafting a mission statement that feels right to you.

_____

_____

_____

_____

A mission statement is not something that you craft perfectly in one day. It typically requires several drafts before you feel that it is done. And even after that you will continue to refine it as you grow on your journey to being mentally tougher. It might take months before you feel entirely comfortable with your mission statement—until you feel that it is a concise expression of your innermost values and directions.

If you feel like it is taking a long time to perfect your statement, don't stress. It is a guide and—like mental toughness—is something that will require work over the course of time.

"We can complain because rose bushes have thorns, or rejoice because thorns have roses."

–Jean-Baptiste Alphonse Karr

CHAPTER 4
STEP 3: PRIORITIZE THE POSITIVE

DURING GAME FOUR of the 2004 American League Championship Series, the Boston Red Sox were down by one run in the ninth inning. Not only that, they were in the midst of an 86-year wait for a World Series championship. And they were down three games to zero. They would go on to become the first and (so far) only baseball team in history to win a postseason series after dropping the first three games. The team won the final eight games of that postseason to end their eight-decade drought.

In game three, the Yankees—their bitter rivals—beat them 19-8. In the ninth inning of game four, the feeling that the Red Sox didn't stand a chance was reinforced by the closing pitcher for the Yankees, Mariano Rivera, the greatest at the position in baseball history. He needed just three outs to put the Yankees in the World Series. After Kevin Millar got a walk, speedster Dave Roberts was sent out to run for him. Back on July 31st of that year, the Red Sox had traded for Roberts from the Los Angeles Dodgers. It was a trade no one noticed, because the Red Sox had traded their franchise icon Nomar Garciaparra on the same day. As Roberts arrived at first base, the voice of legendary base stealer Maury Wills came to him. Wills was a coach with the Dodgers and spoke with him often during spring training.

"I remember Maury Wills on the backfield in Vero Beach," said Roberts. "He said, 'DR, one of these days you're going to have to steal an important base when everyone in the ballpark knows you're gonna steal, but you've got to steal that base and you can't be afraid to steal that base.' So, just kind of trotting out on to the field that night, I was thinking about him."

As Rivera threw his first pitch, Roberts bolted to second. The pitch was perfect for Yankees catcher Jorge Posada—high and a tad outside. The catcher came forward with the fastest release time Red Sox bench coach Brad Mills had ever timed him. The throw was a good one, and shortstop Derek Jeter slapped down the tag. Roberts went head first and was safe— barely. Fenway Park had gone from the quiet optimism provided by the Millar walk to pure excitement.

Roberts would score on the next hit. The teams remained tied until the 12th inning, when David Ortiz hit a home run, sending the Red Sox in a positive direction toward an eventual World Series victory—and two more World Series victories over the course of the next decade. But it all started with Roberts, focusing on the positive in the direst of sports situations. He was a modest player who was called upon to perform a challenging act, even though thousands of people watching and the players on the field knew he was going to do it. He succeeded in the face of adversity by staying positive. In this chapter, we are going to do the same. By focusing on the positive, we are going to get ourselves on the path to mental toughness.

Eviscerate Emotion

As you advance in the direction of your dreams, there will be many times when you will come upon obstacles that will appear bigger than your desire to achieve your specific goal. Emotionally, you will want to give up. Don't let this feeling derail your progress. Instead, we are going to start looking at how you can forge ahead despite the emotional distraction you might encounter along the way.

Often in life we allow emotional distractions to become derailments. We allow our emotions to dictate our outcomes. We allow emotional distractions to take on greater power than they deserve. Don't get me wrong, the distractions of life are real and often difficult to overcome. Remind yourself, however, that each one of them is simply part of your process. The most important thing I can tell you is that it all begins with a simple decision: the decision to move past your emotions and engage your mental toughness mind-set. Emotion can become part of the equation toward building mental toughness, as long as it is balanced with logic. With that in mind, let's review some tools that will help you deal with the emotional distractions in your life.

TOOLS TO HELP YOU GET RID OF NEGATIVE EMOTION

Here are a few tools you can use to begin to shift to a more positive way of thinking. Be easy on yourself, as you will need discipline and continuous effort to learn this new positive behavior.

1. **Step back and look at the situation logically.** Act like you're not emotionally involved, or ask a trusted mentor to help you look at the situation from a neutral perspective. If you force yourself to step outside of the situation, it can be easier to see what is best for you, minus the emotions that often come into play.

2. **Look at metrics and analytics.** Hard numbers and facts can put a situation into perspective like nothing else. This can not only work in business, but also in your personal life as you set certain goals, such as getting out of debt or losing weight. Keep track of everything in a list or spreadsheet so you get the entire picture. Are you really in bad shape, or is that just your negative emotions coming into play? Seeing actual facts in black and white might help you realize you're further ahead in the game than you thought.

3. **Do your research.** Emotional decisions are often made impulsively. If you stop and research a decision before making it, you can rest assured that you are making an informed decision.

4. **Treat your body well.** Exercise can help you clear your mind and de-stress, so make physical activity a daily part of your life. If you like weeding the flowerbed, do it. How about going on a long walk through your neighborhood? And don't forget about eating foods that are good for you, removing or reducing alcohol, and getting a good night's sleep. All

these factor into a positive mind-set so that you can keep negative emotional distractions at bay.

5. **Take a mental break.** To ensure emotions don't get in your way, take a break from the situation. If you're with an employee or a client, excuse yourself from the situation for five to ten minutes. The same goes if it's your spouse or child driving you crazy. If the decision doesn't need to be made right away, give yourself some time to think about it. You'll come back to the situation with a fresh perspective and feel less pressure overall—decreasing the odds of reacting emotionally.

PRACTICE POSITIVE SELF-TALK

If anyone had a good reason to have a "woe is me" attitude, it would be my fellow professional speaker Captain Charlie Plumb. Charlie was a graduate of the United States Naval Academy, a former jet fighter pilot, and a combat veteran with 74 successful missions over Vietnam. He helped start the United States Navy Strike Fighter Tactics Instructor program, known more popularly as Top Gun.

Captain Plumb was shot down over enemy territory on his 75th combat mission, just five days before he was scheduled to return home from Vietnam. He ejected from his F-4 Phantom Jet, parachuted into enemy hands, was taken prisoner, tortured, and survived nearly six years as a prisoner of war.

Think about that for a second. Charlie was scheduled to go home in just five days but instead was suddenly blown out of the sky and his hopes, dreams, and plans evaporated in a heartbeat. Charlie quickly realized, in prison, that those who developed what was described as prison thinking didn't survive. This kind of thinking can best be defined as living in a place where we allow our thinking to be dominated by thoughts like:

» Why did this happen to me?

» What could be worse than this?

» It's not my fault

» I'm a victim!

» I have no control over my destiny

Charlie was held captive in a cell next to a positive thinker named Schumaker. They communicated via Morse code cell to cell, gently tugging out their words on a piece of metal wire between the cells. It was Schumaker who taught Charlie about the concept of "prison thinking."

Charlie quickly learned that those who died most often suffered from negative thinking. In contrast, those who survived did their best to extinguish negative thoughts. He found that these thinkers possessed:

» The power to believe that they would survive

» The power of belief in each other

» The power of positive thinking

» The power to recognize that while his captors captured his body, they could not capture his spirit

» The power of choice

Charlie had to choose which type of thinking he was going to embrace. Initially, he shared how difficult it was to overcome the natural tendency to feel the same human emotions that anyone cast into the same situation might feel. He had to make a conscious decision to choose a winning attitude and to practice daily positive self-talk. He worked tirelessly at not only surviving, but also at becoming the highest possible version of himself— because his life depended on it.

One concept that Charlie shared the day we first met is something that I have practiced ever since because it has made a profound and meaningful difference in my life. Charlie shared that we all have moments of self-doubt; those times when we are feeling insecure about ourselves. He said when we are feeling that way that we should never say our self-doubt out loud. For example, don't say: "I'm not a good cook," "I am too old," or "They will never hire me." Why? Because as I noted before, when we share those limiting thoughts of self-doubt out loud, our brain actually hears them twice: once through the inner dialogue and then once again through our ears.

When we take our limiting thoughts, put them into words, and then say them out loud, we reinforce and strengthen them. We make them more intense because when we take something that was once only a thought and convert it into a word, we give it a second life. Any positive or negative affirmation is reinforced when it is spoken out loud. Words have power. Choose them wisely.

PEP YOURSELF UP

Are you feeling down or unmotivated? Are you trying to get ready for a job interview, a special event like a speech, or reaching a goal? Here are some of my favorite ideas for lifting yourself up:

TALK TO YOURSELF LIKE A FRIEND. Just as you would do for a friend who is struggling with self-doubt, give yourself a pep talk to create and reinforce mental toughness.

TREAT YOURSELF. If you find yourself being extremely critical, incentivize yourself. Are you struggling to finish your work for that meeting tomorrow? Tell yourself that you will enjoy some TV time or treat yourself to a latte from your favorite coffee shop once you're done. You don't have to break the bank to treat yourself well.

WATCH AN INSPIRING VIDEO. There are thousands of motivating videos on the Internet. Find and save your favorites to watch when you are feeling unsure or unmotivated.

WRITE DOWN WHAT YOU ARE GRATEFUL FOR. Write down three things that you are grateful for *right now* (I am healthy; my children are safe; I have a roof over my head; etc.). It's amazing how gratitude can lift you up.

Activate Optimism

Mentally tough people are resilient in large part because they turn negative thoughts into productive reality. Each day the news tells us what's wrong with the world. The lyrics of many songs are filled with hate-filled rants that can do great harm to your psyche. Combine that with the daily struggles we each have paying for our expenses and balancing our work with pleasure and it's no surprise that so many of us have a hard time carving out a life of positivity and optimism.

OPTIMISM TRAINING

The United States military offers a resilience-building program designed to increase mental toughness, put together by a team of researchers at the University of Pennsylvania. The military has created this program because they aim to make soldiers rugged in body and mind.

The key lesson that the drill sergeants who have received the training are sharing with their soldiers is that mental toughness comes from thinking like an optimist. The 10-day training program gives participants a keen understanding of how to toughen the mind, something that top scientists and military minds alike view as a necessity for the world's greatest military force.

Setting expectations is essential to activating optimism. Expect that you will be happy. Expect that you will be optimistic. Expect that you will be mentally tough. Here are some ideas to help you stay optimistic:

Highlight the positive. Keep a journal and take a few minutes each day to write down some of the great things that have happened to you. And don't just make it all about yourself! Share the love by telling your neighbor just how awesome they are or letting your family know how blessed you are to have them. Try to give love away—the harder you try the more it will just keep coming back to you.

Nix the negative. If you find yourself turning on a loop of negativity, immediately begin repeating your favorite mantra out loud until you cancel the negative vibe. My favorite inspirational speaker, Les Brown, repeats the phrase, "I am blessed and highly favored."

Volunteer. There are lots of groups that need your time and talents. Try to share your gifts at least once a month. The more you give of yourself, the more you will receive from those you serve. Optimism grows when we are in service to those who need us most.

Maintain active engagement. Become actively engaged in your spiritual, physical, and emotional well-being. Most people lead lives of passive engagement, so shake things up. Learn to play the guitar, enter a chili cook-off, or deliver a reading at your church. The more actively engaged you are, the happier and more optimistic you will be.

THE HEALTH BENEFITS OF OPTIMISM

Researchers at the Mayo Clinic have identified the health benefits that positive thinking and optimism may provide, including:

- Increased longevity
- Lower rates of depression
- Lower levels of distress
- Greater resistance to the common cold
- Better psychological and physical well-being
- Better cardiovascular health

Seek solitude. We are each inundated with noise and technology every day. Carve out a minimum of 10 minutes each day to be with just you. No music, no sounds, no talking. Imagine lying in a cool stream as clear water passes through your body, filtering out all the angst from your day. This time will rest and rejuvenate your mind and body, giving you the strength you need to expel negative thoughts and focus on staying optimistic.

Studies have shown that optimism can be instilled by something as simple as having people think about the best possible outcomes in various areas of their lives. Remember, you have the power right now to adjust your thinking by simply making the choice to be more optimistic.

Visualize Positive Results

Studies show that visualizing success helps bring it to fruition. Here's what we know about visualization, how to do it, and why it works for developing mental toughness.

TD Bank surveyed more than 1,100 people and 500 small business owners nationwide to learn about their visualization practices. What they learned is that those who create a vision board (or a less formally organized collection of images and photos) that relate to their goals are almost twice as confident that they'll achieve them as those who don't visualize their goals in some way. In fact, 67 percent of those surveyed believe that pictures of their goals will improve the odds they will achieve them.

It might sound silly, but think about small business owners as a group; they started their businesses because they had a vision and chose to follow it. By keeping their eyes on the big picture, they were able to successfully push their plan forward. Think of yourself as the small business owner of your life; you can do your best to visualize the best results for yourself. You are your best advocate and visualizing positive results for your life is a major step toward becoming mentally tough.

WRITE IN YOUR SUCCESS

Jack Canfield, the co-author of the *Chicken Soup for the Soul* series, which has over 500 million copies in print in over 40 languages, recommends that you create a picture or visual representation for every goal you have. When he was writing the very first book in the bestselling series, he scanned a copy of the *New York Times* bestseller list onto his computer and typed *Chicken Soup for the Soul* into the number one position on the list. He then printed several copies and hung them around his office. Less than two years later, the book occupied the real top spot and stayed there for over a year. You're probably thinking, "If only it was that easy!" The truth is that visualizing your success and keeping those positive thoughts in mind can really make a difference.

Positivity is contagious. An increase in positivity will have a direct impact on mental toughness and the best part is, positivity can be learned. By using the exercises in this chapter, you can help positivity become a constant part of your daily life through habits and practice. Shawn Achor, the *New York Times* bestselling author of *Before Happiness* and *The Happiness Advantage*, said that when you are happy your brain has a "happy advantage" and it performs better, intelligence rises, your creativity gets a boost, and energy levels surge. There is positivity within you and it is important to harness as much as you can in order to grow mentally tough. It is a choice that can lead to success in everyday life.

Getting rid of negative emotions, activating optimism, and utilizing visualization are designed to help you prioritize the positive in your life. With these tools at the ready, you are one step closer to obtaining mental toughness.

"We can let the circum-
stances of our lives
harden us so that we
become increasingly
resentful and afraid, or
we can let them soften
us, and make us kinder.
We always have the
choice."

–Dalai Lama

CHAPTER 5
STEP 4: FLEX YOUR FLEXIBILITY

MENTALLY TOUGH PEOPLE are able to recover from setbacks quickly. The term "roll with the punches" originated in the sport of boxing. It is a technique that tells boxers to step back or to one side as they are being punched so that they lessen the impact and absorb a fraction of the full force of the hit. In mental toughness training, we roll with the punches by choosing a mind-set that allows us to be resilient and recover from setbacks quickly and confidently.

Setbacks are simply opportunities in disguise. That's exactly how Walt Disney perceived his setbacks during the 1930s. On the brink of bankruptcy, Disney mortgaged his home to release the film *Snow White and the Seven Dwarfs*. And what a smart move, since the blockbuster allowed his company to put his financial woes in the rearview mirror.

Even Bill Gates failed when he was on a team that launched a company called Traf-O-Data. Their business became obsolete in a heartbeat when the State of Washington began to offer the exact same service they were working on for free. Even though it could be seen as a failure, the experience was seminal in helping launch Microsoft.

How did these two titans rebound from their setbacks? By maintaining a flexible mind-set.

It may seem impossible to prepare for the unknown, but there are steps you can take to get ready for whatever life throws at you. It is all about developing the proper mind-set. Your ability to do this is in direct proportion to how effective you are at remaining flexible.

We achieve this vital flexibility by utilizing what I refer to as a neutral positioning statement (NPS), a mantra you repeat to yourself to reframe how you perceive and process even the most difficult circumstance or situation. It allows you to look at any event and remove the emotion connected to it. It is by reframing our perception of an event, obstacle, or circumstance and not seeing it as simply "good" or "bad" that we become more flexible and equipped to handle and manage adversity.

For example, if you have to deliver a speech to your company and are not comfortable with public speaking, your neutral positioning statement (NPS) might be, "I will boost my confidence by creating a presentation that I am excited to share and that will help others." It is important to practice this neutral positioning technique if you are going to be able to craft a fine-tuned, flexible mind-set.

Change with the Circumstances

Mentally tough people are familiar with the old adage, "The only constant is change." While it is true, they have learned not only how to accept and adapt to change, but to also thrive with it.

The 2016 movie *Hacksaw Ridge* is based on the true story of Pfc. Desmond T. Doss, a soldier who won the Congressional Medal of Honor despite refusing to bear arms on religious grounds during World War II. Even though he was harassed for his pacifist views by his fellow soldiers, his willingness to serve was exemplary. He was undaunted by the barrage of continual insults hurled his way and eventually went on to become a medic. While serving in 1944 during the Battle of Okinawa, he saved the lives of 75 men while under heavy fire, earning the respect of those who once belittled him.

What Doss possessed was an exceedingly high level of grit, determination, and mental toughness. While he did not have the ability to change the circumstance, he did possess the ability to change within the circumstance. He accepted war for what it was, quickly adapted to it, and then made an impactful difference. His ability to change allowed him to thrive even during war by learning new ways to adapt, overcome, and improvise. These three qualities are crucial for those who want to achieve mental toughness.

Like Doss, you need to be able to change as your circumstances change in order to become mentally tougher. How?

» Pick up a book on the subject matter to gain insights.

» Find a mentor who you respect and ask for guidance.

» Meditate. There is a good chance you already know how to change. Quiet time may allow the solution to come to the surface.

» Imitate. Success leaves clues. Find out what someone else did in a similar situation and mimic their strategy.

HOW HUMOR HELPS

Changing circumstances can be unsettling, but humor helps mitigate its negative effects. Scientifically, we know that laughter is a large and powerful force. Our bodies release dopamine and endorphins so that we can cope with stress and see problems in new ways. A Stanford University study found that subjects who looked at horrifying images and then improvised jokes reported increases in positive emotions and decreases in negative ones. The researchers concluded that, "If you are able to teach people to be more playful, to look at the absurdities of life as humorous, you see some increase in well-being." Try out your funny bone and see if it helps you adapt to new circumstances. It should.

Learn to adapt to your situation and try different approaches until you find one that works. You may have to step out of your comfort zone, too (and we'll go into that further in chapter 6).

Prepare to be Flexible

One of the best ways to handle times of uncertainty is to prepare for them. By expecting change to occur, you can learn to be more flexible, adaptable, and resilient. The great news for us is that experts in behavior science view mental flexibility not as a personality trait but as a set of behaviors that can be modified or changed. As we become more flexible, we often uncover areas of opportunity that previously had not been available to us because of positive shifts in our perspective.

Here are a few strategies to consider for improving your flexibility:

Alpha awareness: Do you have to be at the top of the food chain in everything you do? If so, consider dialing it back a notch. To practice flexibility, change the pace by letting others take on the roles and responsibilities that you normally would take on for things you don't truly enjoy. Instead of taking charge, simply look for ways to support and encourage others.

Compromise coach: Consider how willing you are to compromise. Flexible people are resilient because they don't always have to get their way. Become your own compromise coach and look out for opportunities to work well with others by creating win-win situations.

Foster flexibility: Improving your mental flexibility is no different from stretching before working out. With time and practice your mental flexibility will follow and your stress level will be reduced.

Reward yourself: There is a good chance as you move forward in your mental flexibility work that you will sometimes revert back to inflexible patterns. It will happen, so don't beat yourself up. Simply get back on track and reward yourself in small ways when you catch yourself doing something right. Being flexible starts with being flexible with yourself.

Failure is not fatal: Becoming more flexible is a great goal to aspire to. It will pay health and wellness dividends that will help you ease the burden of life. When you stumble on those times where you fall short of the intended goal, take a deep breath, release, and then move on. With time and practice your behaviors will change, as will your outlook on life.

Recover Quickly

Mentally tough people don't wallow in would have, could have, or should have. They turn mistakes, failures, and adversity around quickly without ever becoming a victim. Regardless of what it is that comes crashing down on your world, whether it is a crushing defeat in business, divorce, a health scare, or a parenting challenge, commit to getting to the recovery stage as quickly as possible. Here are four steps to help make that happen:

1. DON'T ALLOW YOURSELF TO BECOME A VICTIM

Regardless of the mistake, setback, adversity, or circumstance that confronts you, refuse to play the role as the victim. Rather than view your challenge as a catastrophe in that moment, look at it as simply a new chapter. By shifting your perspective, you will prevent yourself from becoming a victim of circumstance.

The longer you remain a victim of your own thoughts and perceptions, the longer it will take you to recover. Mental toughness is not about avoiding extreme difficulty; it is about how to recover from the challenges we face rapidly and effectively. This is different from letting yourself grieve and mourn. You need to express those emotions when something truly bad happens, but don't turn the negative feelings toward yourself. For example, when a loved one passes away, mourn the person that they were but don't wallow in the fact that you didn't spend as much time as you wanted with them when they were alive.

Everyone experiences mistakes and failures. Mentally tough people don't allow themselves to become the victim or to be defined by these negative experiences.

2. CONTROL WHAT YOU CAN

Developing a mental toughness mind-set is a forward-thinking, solution-based alternative. When a crisis happens, immediately put your thoughts and actions on a track where you are looking for ways to improve the situation, rather than trying to figure out all the reasons why something went wrong. Remain in control so that your reactions to stressful situations don't turn you into a self-imposed victim.

3. PRE-PLAY THE FUTURE INSTEAD OF REPLAYING THE PAST

Rather than spending needless energy replaying a never-ending negative loop of the past, trying to figure out how the situation could have been avoided, pre-play the future by visualizing the path you will use to navigate your way out of the adverse situation. This technique forces you to remain forward-focused, looking for a solution to the problem.

First, specify what aspects of the current situation you can directly influence to change the course of the adverse circumstance. Second, visualize the tools you will use to navigate your way to a better place. Last, collaborate. Who can you enlist as part of your team to gain greater insights? When you engage the life experiences of others and utilize their perspectives and perceptions, there is a very good chance their time-tested tools will help you recover quickly from your adversity.

4. MOVE ON

Mentally tough people do not allow suffering and mistakes to define them, shape them, and rob them of living a life they want. After you reach out to others for support and make space for yourself to roll with the punches and recover from setbacks, you will have a decision to make: Will you see stepping outside of your comfort zone as an obstacle, or will you decide to use it to propel you in a new direction?

MANAGE DISTRACTIONS

Don't let your distractions become derailments. You will have interruptions every day on your way to achieving your mental toughness goals; that's just part of the process. The key is to not let those distractions completely derail you during the journey.

The milkshake you just had, it's a distraction, so don't let it derail your weight loss goals. You could even view it as a part of treating yourself. The deflating conversation you had with someone about starting your own business is merely a distraction, so keep moving. Want to be a motivational speaker? Don't let bad feedback after just one speech derail you.

Distractions are something designed to throw you off course on your way to your goal. They are reminders of how easy it would be to lose focus, slow down, and even quit. When your distractions seem to be getting the best of you, put your blinders on and power through them to become mentally tougher.

Successful people have the ability to absorb the unexpected and remain mentally tough. They are even able to maintain humor when situations become scary. If something isn't going well or doesn't turn out as expected, they remain flexible in their approach and look for new ways to solve the problem. Just like a quarterback faced with a broken play, mentally tough people may have to decide quickly on a different way to get the ball down the field.

In addition, you must continually be open to re-educating yourself, even in the basics, of what it means to be mentally tough. That means reinforcing the steps discussed in the previous chapter.

"Step so far out of your comfort zone that you forget how to get back."

–Anonymous

CHAPTER 6
STEP 5: STEP OUTSIDE YOUR COMFORT ZONE

LEARNING TO BE mentally tough can be difficult at times. And one of the best—and often hardest—ways to develop mental toughness is to stretch yourself to the point of discomfort. As the Navy SEALs say, "Get comfortable being uncomfortable."

To illustrate that point, consider the BUD/S (basic underwater demolition) training that Navy SEALs go through. If they are fortunate enough to pass the rigorous PST (physical screening test), they are immediately assigned to BUD/S and on their way to training, where each candidate will run through a battery of tests designed to try their physical prowess as well as emotional resilience. There is no room for failure—you pass or you're out.

In an exercise called surf torture, the men are ordered to link arms and then lie down on their backs with their heads and torsos partially submerged in the pounding surf. They lie there until they reach a mild level of hypothermia, then are ordered to get up and run to the sand dunes and completely cover their wet bodies with sand—and then do it all over again. They do this daily before taking on whatever tasks are required of them for the day. Why? So they will stay focused on what they need to accomplish, regardless of pain or discomfort.

My personal favorite set of exercises that show how truly hard Navy SEALs train is called drown-proofing. With arms and legs bound, candidates jump into a 9-foot-deep pool. Once in the water they have to perform a variety of skills:

Bottom bounce: The test taker sinks to the bottom and bounces off hard enough that they can rise to the surface, breathe, and repeat. It sounds easy but with your hands bound it is difficult.

Float: Doing a dead man float is not that tough—except if your hands and feet are tied.

Swim 100 meters: The only way to swim with your hands and feet tied is by doing a dolphin kick, which is extremely difficult.

Front and back flip: After swimming, the test taker has to perform a front and back flip without using their hands for stability.

Mask retrieval: By the way, you cannot use a mask or goggles with this drill. The final drill is for the test taker to dive down and retrieve a mask that is sitting at the bottom of the pool. They must grab it with their teeth and bring it to the surface while holding it with their mouths.

Each test is designed to see if a trainee has the grit to thrive under adverse conditions. To be a Navy SEAL means you are among the elite, and therefore the training relies heavily on testing the mental capacity of each candidate, as well their physical limits. To become a member of this elite squad and to maximize the potential of the Navy SEAL training regimen, physical training is important but developing mental toughness in uncomfortable and unfamiliar situations is even more so.

The benefits of stepping outside of your comfort zone are immense. Challenging yourself pushes you to dig deeper and excavate an untapped reservoir of knowledge and resources that will pay dividends and growth opportunities that will change your life forever. Taking risks, even if you fall short of your intended goal, will help you learn lessons that will enable you to eventually accomplish your ultimate goals.

Here's an important secret: Stepping outside your comfort zone will be easier if you stop caring about what other people think and if you stop worrying about the possibility of failing. In fact, stepping outside your comfort zone will often put you in a place where you may fail—let that be okay. Failing is an important first step on your way to a greater goal. Helen Keller put it best when she said, "Life is either a daring adventure or nothing at all." If you are not failing, you are not growing.

Get Comfortable Being Uncomfortable

Being uncomfortable isn't any fun. But mentally tough people put themselves in uncomfortable situations because doing so teaches them how to handle stress, solve problems, and think critically. You must begin to do the things you don't want to do if you want to become the person you have the capacity to be. The fact is, if you want to make big things happen in your life, you must begin to get comfortable with being uncomfortable. And that means that you need to eliminate the word *quit* from your vocabulary.

You can't get mentally stronger if you stay in your comfort zone at all times. When you're willing to move out of your comfort zone you will:

Have an easier time dealing with new and unexpected changes. Brené Brown, a research professor at the University of Houston and a *New York Times* bestselling author, explains that one of the worst things we can do is pretend that fear and uncertainty don't exist. By taking risks in a controlled fashion and challenging yourself to do things you normally wouldn't do, you can experience some of that uncertainty in a controlled, manageable environment. Learning to live outside your comfort zone when you choose to can prepare you for those times when you're forced out of it by unexpected life changes.

Find it easier to push your boundaries in the future. Once you start making an effort to adapt to changing circumstances, it gets easier over time and you'll become accustomed to that state of optimal anxiety. Productive discomfort becomes more normal to you, and you'll find yourself willing to push further before your performance falls off. As you challenge yourself, your comfort zone adjusts so what was difficult and anxiety-inducing becomes easier as you repeat it.

Be more productive. Comfort kills productivity because without the sense of unease that comes from having deadlines and expectations, we tend to phone it in and do the minimum required to get by. We lose the drive and ambition to do more and learn new things. We also fall into the work trap, where we feign that we are busy as a way to stay in our comfort zones and avoid doing new things. Pushing your personal boundaries can help you hit your stride sooner, get more done, and find smarter ways to work.

The benefits you get after stepping outside of your comfort zone on your journey to becoming mentally tougher can linger. You'll discover the overall self-improvement you get through the skills you're learning, the new foods you're trying, the new country you're visiting, and the new job you're interviewing for.

Case Western Reserve University professor Richard Boyatzis's research suggests that being able to change with your circumstances predicts satisfaction with your life and career, as well as career success. This was based on a study that tracked a group of MBA students 19 years after they graduated. Those who ranked high in adaptability as students were the most satisfied and successful almost two decades later. The findings of the research were clear: adaptable people meet new challenges with ease and are comfortable with the uncertainty that reaching for goals can bring.

Ask yourself this question: When was the last time you tried something new? If the answer is, "It's been forever" or "I can't even remember," then it's time to step out of your comfort zone.

Do yourself a favor, though, and do not try to take on something dramatic for the first time. For the time being, start by taking baby steps toward building your ability to get comfortable with being uncomfortable. For example, try brushing your teeth with the opposite hand or walking up the stairs backward. Too easy? How about getting up at 4 a.m. to start your day or taking a cold shower? This will test how comfortable you are with being uncomfortable.

Once you master those tests, try something a bit more challenging. What about using your voice to stand up at a Board of Education meeting at your child's school? Or volunteering to run a local fundraiser? Putting yourself in a new situation triggers your brain to release dopamine, which in simple terms is the main chemical of pleasure. And it gets released by the brain when you experience completely new things.

Whatever your mental toughness objectives are, stretching the limits of your comfort is vital to gaining it. Identify your specific goal and break it down into its physical and mental parts. Work in both areas as you continue to cultivate and nurture a new, more powerful mind-set. Few people enjoy the feeling of being uncomfortable. The challenge is to get past that initial negative feeling, so you can grow and benefit from your discomfort.

Use these five steps to help get more comfortable with being uncomfortable:

1. **Simply start.** It's a fact that many people will never step up to the starting line. They will spend years thinking about all the reasons why the situation is not just right to start a new business, go back to college, run their first marathon, or leave a job that doesn't work for them. The greatest fear is the fear (and discomfort) of the unknown. Whatever your goal is, you must begin. Once you have crossed that threshold, the road map will often fall into place—but it all starts with you making the decision to start.

2. **Don't quit.** Once you begin, don't give up. Many dreams die when a person steps out to follow a dream and quickly finds out how much work it entails and how uncomfortable it can get. I refer to this moment as the circle of failure. You get excited and your adrenaline starts to run through your veins when a new opportunity comes into your orbit. But getting involved will require hard work, knowledge, and perseverance. Once many people hit this point, the discomfort tells them to quit and to start something new. But moving on to another endeavor won't solve the problem since there will always be uncomfortable and difficult moments in whatever you do. It's better to forge ahead and get comfortable with

being uncomfortable until you push past the difficulty and finally see some success.

3. **Fake it until you make it.** Fear kills more dreams than failure ever will. When you find that the fear of the unknown or of failing is starting to take over, visualize yourself finding success in your goal or repeat a positive mantra. Envisioning yourself crossing the finish line or being showered with compliments can be enough to get yourself over the hump so you move forward toward your ultimate goal.

4. **Share your journey.** One of the best ways to power through your discomfort is to begin taking the journey with other likeminded people instead of going it alone. By taking on the challenge with others and creating a support network, you have the benefit of sharing war stories and humor that only those on the inside will understand. The camaraderie you share will help you forge relationships that can last a lifetime—not to mention help you over any hump that comes your way now or in the future.

5. **Recognize your progress and repeat.** Track your progress and celebrate the change you see in yourself. Once you experience success with one challenge, you will feel more confident taking on another. Build your confidence by going through the uncomfortable experience again if necessary so you can experience and see your progress in real time. The more you perform the same activity, the more your confidence will grow. Confidence—like mental toughness—is a tangible attribute that is in your control. It comes from practice and repetition.

A NEW CHALLENGE EVERY DAY

Why is challenging yourself important in developing a mental toughness mind-set? In a few words: to be able to live your life to the fullest. To grow your mental toughness mind-set, try something that challenges you every day. Consider doing what Michelle Poler did. She gave herself a challenge: face 100 fears in 100 days. Her challenges ranged from the mundane, like holding a cat and riding a mechanical bull, to the daunting, such as delivering a TEDx speech and rappelling off a cliff.

When we challenge ourselves, we tap into a reservoir of potential that lies dormant within us. The more we challenge ourselves, the more we gain access to that reservoir. You will quickly build confidence in your abilities as well as grow your capacity to live the life you are capable of living. Mastering a mental toughness mind-set comes with time by challenging yourself and stretching your limits. The courage you forge today will be the mental toughness mind-set of your tomorrow. Today, begin with small challenges like:

- Applying for your dream job

- Signing up for a new workout class

- Unplugging for 24 hours

- Eating new foods for an entire day

- Connecting with someone you admire

- Calling a potential new client

Move Past Fear

If we allow it, fear and anxiety can hold us back from trying new things, challenging ourselves, and achieving big goals. The fear of getting hurt, being judged, or failing is powerful. The fear of the unknown is real. Fear can prevent people from becoming who they have the capacity to be. With that in mind, it's important to understand the root of our fear so that we can create a strategy to deal with it.

If fear of failure is what is holding you back, consider the life of Abraham Lincoln, who is regarded as one of the greatest leaders in history. As a young man, he went to war as a captain and returned as a private, the lowest rank. He failed at business on several attempts, went bankrupt more than once, and was defeated over two dozen times in political campaigns. He could have easily allowed his fear of his past failures to control his destiny, but he didn't.

As president, he was able to make tough decisions while under immense pressure. Despite mourning the loss of his son and caring for his grieving wife, he was still able to lead the United States out of the Civil War and abolish slavery.

Despite numerous, very real failures, Lincoln pushed through his past and took his rightful place in history.

Another president, Calvin Coolidge, is credited with this quote about moving past fear: "Nothing in the world can take the place of persistence. Talent will not; nothing is more common than unsuccessful men with talent. Genius will not; unrewarded genius is almost a proverb. Education will not; the world is full of educated derelicts. Persistence and determination are omnipotent. The slogan 'press on' has solved and always will solve the problems of the human race."

There are three primary options you can choose from when dealing with fear as it pertains to your dreams and goals. It's important to honestly assess how you most often respond to fear as it presents itself.

1. **Run.** The problem with running from your fears is that at some point there is a good chance that the decision to run, especially if it prevents

you from achieving an important goal, may cause you to lose your zest for life. Not following your dreams can eventually lead to despair or even depression.

2. **Do nothing.** This is when you sit on the sidelines even though you have a goal that may be important to you. Your fear and anxiety paralyze you. You don't run from your fear or act on it. You simply wait, trying to convince yourself that you will act on achieving your goal when conditions are just right. Studies have shown that people who are highly afraid of failing are more likely to procrastinate. The transition position, as I call it, is filled with "what if" self-talk: What if I don't succeed? What if I can't find the financing I need? What if I let my family down? Nothing paralyzes us like "what if."

3. **Attack your fear.** As I've mentioned in previous chapters, mental tough-ness is a mind-set that allows you to boldly advance toward a goal regardless of fear, pain, or circumstance. As your mental toughness mind-set strengthens, you will begin to attack your fear on the way to your goals. Almost always, when you move past your fear, you will find that it was not a leap that got you past your fear, but instead a simple step over a threshold that you had previously made bigger in your mind than it actually is.

Mentally tough people know that whatever the fear, they must confront it head-on to move past it. These people experience the same fears and anxieties as everyone else; it's how they move past those fears that helps them reach their goals. Mentally tough people ask themselves the following questions to move past their fear:

1. **What am I afraid of?** This is the most important question mentally tough people should be able to answer—and quickly. Identifying why you are fearful and acknowledging that your fear is real is the first step to understanding what is holding you back. Write a list of what you feel are the greatest fears that are holding you back. Beneath that, write a list of possible solutions and tools you can use to help move past those fears.

2. **Why am I beating myself up?** Feeling bad about yourself or wallowing in self-pity when faced with a fear is not going to help you move past it. Remember that fear is a natural protective mechanism, so you shouldn't feel bad about experiencing it. It's letting those fears take control over your life that is the main concern.

3. **Is this a rational fear?** The key to moving past your fears quickly is to identify if your fear is rational or irrational. For example, fear of swimming with white sharks is a rational fear designed to protect you; however, fear of making a speech at a company event or your best friend's wedding is irrational, in the sense that it is not life-threatening and is a fear that you can, with help, work through.

4. **What will your future look like?** What if you don't step forward and face your fear? Will you be okay with that? I had an employee years ago who wanted to try to play major league baseball, but he was scared of the possibility of not being good enough. As we talked, he quickly concluded that he would be more scared of the prospect of not ever knowing if he had what it took to make it in the big leagues. He ended up moving to Florida for spring training camp and found after a month that, in fact, he didn't have the skills he needed to compete at that level. While he was disappointed, he was at peace knowing he had gone as far as he needed to go with this specific dream. He had given it his all. So before you give up on a dream, think carefully about what your future will look like if you don't face your fear.

Refresh, Renew, and Revive

After reviewing our five steps, it might be hard for you to imagine that people who are really tough actually take the time to meditate or focus on breathing, but they do. While we have committed ourselves to being determined as well as flexible in our quest for mental toughness, we also need to give ourselves time to relax. In fact, practicing this type of self-care on a regular basis is vital to being mentally tough. Remember the three R's: refresh, renew, and revive—which all lead to the big R: resilience.

According to Ferris Jabr of *Scientific American*, "Research on naps, meditation, nature walks and the habits of exceptional artists and athletes reveals how mental breaks increase productivity, replenish attention, solidify memories and encourage creativity."

What is it that you can do to help yourself slow down? What gives you a sense of renewal? Once you find this out, do it early and often. Don't wait for the next crisis in your life to remind you that you need to take care of yourself. Instead, create the discipline needed to slow down and carve out the time to do it. Here are some proven ways to recharge and at the same time become tougher every single day of your life:

Set office hours. When you physically leave your office at the end of the day, do your best to leave the stresses of the workplace there. If you happen to work from home, make sure you designate one area as your office so that most of your house can be a "work-free" zone. When your workday is done, make time to indulge in your hobbies, listen to a favorite podcast, read, or unwind any way you want.

Take breaks. Did you know that your brain can only effectively focus for 90 to 120 minutes before it needs a break? Experts recommend taking a break during regular intervals to boost your mental energy during the workday. That means you shouldn't feel guilty about taking several small breaks throughout the day.

Remember that your phone is your friend. You might think of your phone as an enemy of relaxation and mental toughness, but if utilized correctly it can be an extremely valuable resource. In addition to using your phone as a timer during work breaks, there are numerous apps you can download to help you relax, meditate, and more.

Get enough sleep. In order to stay mentally focused, it is essential that you get enough sleep at night. Recharging with eight hours of sleep every night will put you in the position to be as mentally tough as possible.

Being mentally tough is about having the courage to practice and develop habits that will help you be the most successful and happy person you can be. Just as you have committed yourself to developing the focus, determination, and confidence necessary to succeed in all areas of your life, you need to commit yourself to rest and rejuvenation.

You now have the tools to develop your mental toughness by stretching yourself to the point of discomfort. You understand that you can't get stronger by staying in your comfort zone and that you need to practice a positive mind-set so that optimism becomes a regular part of your life. And, of course, there's the all-important rest and rejuvenation part of the equation. Now that you have the tools, let's explore in chapter 7 how to bring it all together.

"Inaction breeds doubt and fear. Action breeds confidence and courage. If you want to conquer fear, do not sit home and think about it. Go out and get busy."

—Dale Carnegie

CHAPTER 7
MOVING AHEAD WITH MENTAL TOUGHNESS

CONGRATULATIONS! YOU ARE now the mentally toughest person in the world.

Only kidding—the rewarding work has just begun. It's now time to practice and hone your new skills with the program below.

You know the five steps and how to implement them individually. Let's use a common scenario to walk through the steps and show how they fit together to create a mental toughness program.

The situation: Your partner asks for a divorce.

Divorce can be a difficult, life-changing event. Even in the best of breakups, navigating the process can be an emotional rollercoaster ride filled with fear, anxiety, and confusion. But it doesn't have to be. You can use the five steps to mental toughness to make the transition smoother, regardless of what your partner may do.

Remind yourself out loud that mental toughness is the mind-set that will boldly advance you toward a goal regardless of fear, pain, or circumstance. Your goal is to get to other side of your divorce emotionally intact and feeling whole. Keep in mind that you will be tested at every turn to see if you are mentally tough enough to stay on track and forge ahead.

The important thing to remember is that how you process the experience of divorce will have a huge impact on your life moving forward. For that reason, you need to process it in a way that minimizes the potential negative impact it has on you, your former partner, and your children.

Initially, give yourself permission to be angry, confused, and hurt. Whatever you are feeling is normal. It will take time and hard work to move past your pain. Remember, though, that you are the only one who has full control over your healing process. You can expedite or delay the healing process based on how you process your divorce (or any life-changing event).

Let's look at how to process divorce using the five steps to mental toughness. Here is how I am approaching the situation that I'm in now.

Step 1: Let Go and Take Charge

1. **Accept.** Accept the fact that life is going to change. Many of the changes will not be easy. Acceptance will keep you forward-focused and away from a negative loop that holds your thoughts in the past on what might have been.

2. **Decide.** You are the only one who can determine if your divorce will be a catastrophe or a new chapter. If you process your divorce as a catastrophe your experience will paralyze you. You will be focused on circumstances that no longer matter and are beyond your control. You could then get locked in a negative loop for years. Take charge of the present by treating it as a new chapter. Commit to looking for opportunities to grow, heal, and improve through the experience.

3. **Fake control.** Act like you're in control, even though internally you may feel that you are anything but in control. Use a mantra that speaks to you and repeat it out loud, early and often. When you repeat your mantra over and over again, your mind can only focus on the positive words, drowning out the spiraling loop of negativity you may find yourself caught in. (For example, I repeat the words, "It will be okay.")

4. **Forgive.** Forgive yourself as well as your former spouse. Forgiveness is one of the most powerful tools you can implement to heal. Remind yourself that you are forgiving your former partner so that you will receive the benefit of letting go.

5. **Get help.** Get professional help dealing with the pain and uncertainty. A good therapist can help you reframe and adjust your perspective if it is holding you back. Identify excuses you have made regarding your marriage and uncover behaviors that may be stopping you from moving forward.

6. **Let go.** Create a letting go ceremony. Begin to work on releasing the pain of the past in favor of gaining a bright and optimistic future. Repeat the wise words of Nelson Mandela after spending 27 years in prison: "As I walked out the door toward the gate that would lead to my freedom, I knew if I didn't leave my bitterness and hatred behind, I'd still be in prison."

Step 2: Create a Mission Statement

1. **Identify what you want** for yourself, your children, and your former spouse as you move through the process of divorce. Create a mission statement in 40 words or less that is specific to your divorce. A specific personal mission statement will help you stay on track when you are going though moments of fear, doubt, and uncertainty.

    Here is mine: "I am committed to working collaboratively with my former spouse to ensure our transition is as compassionate, positive, and supportive as it can be, for myself, our children, and my former partner."

    Your personal mission statement will encourage you to work at becoming the highest possible version of yourself while you navigate this time of uncertainty. The transition will be difficult. Your personal mission statement will help you minimize the potential negative impact the event has on your physical, spiritual, and emotional well-being.

2. **Maintain your moral compass.** Regardless of what others may be doing around you, commit to living an authentic lifestyle by following your moral compass.

3. **Define success for you.** Some of your neighbors, friends, and even family members are going to judge you. So what?! Use the So What Method and move on. Let go of any shame or embarrassment. Simply follow your core beliefs and get busy creating an empowered future for yourself and your family.

4. **Set goals.** As you move through the process of divorce, focus on setting forward-focused goals that inspire and motivate you to become the highest possible version of yourself, rather than slipping into resentment, fear, and anger. Forward-focused goals will help you stay on track and work toward a journey that will be solution- and healing-centered versus pain- and anger-based. Take a cooking class, become a Zumba instructor, or learn Spanish. Make sure you have a goal-specific, benefit-rich game plan to work toward every day.

Step 3: Prioritize the Positive

1. **Step back.** Act like you're not emotionally involved. Step outside of the situation. You'll be able to more easily see what is best for you when you emotionally detach.

2. **Activate optimism.** Become actively engaged in your physical, spiritual, and emotional well-being in new ways. Hang with people who lift you up. Start a new hobby.

3. **Self-care.** Practice positive self-care. Work out regularly. Get good sleep. Meditate or pray. Reduce or eliminate alcohol, a poor diet, negative people, and negative conversations.

4. **Visualize.** Visualize what you believe an optimal divorce would look like. Work at creating that experience regardless of what is thrown at you. Focus on what positive steps you can take in the future versus what negative steps your partner took in the past.

Step 4: Flex Your Flexibility

1. **Prepare.** In divorce, things will often not go as planned. Prepare for the unexpected. When your initial plans go awry, have a plan in place to help you respond logically, rather than emotionally. Spend as little time as possible dwelling on what went wrong and commit to finding ways to improve the situation in the moment. Adapt, overcome, and improvise.

2. **Compromise.** Trying to change your spouse will only lead to additional stress. Instead, look for opportunities to compromise as a stress reduction method.

3. **Recover.** Don't allow yourself to become a victim in your divorce. The longer you engage in a pity party the longer it will take you to recover and move on.

4. **Find humor.** Teach yourself to become more playful. Go to a comedy club with friends. Watch videos that make you laugh. Take a class in improv or stand up.

5. **Use neutral positioning statements (NPS).** Reframe the adverse circumstance into something that is neither good nor bad; rather, it simply just is. You become more flexible by removing emotion and dealing with the situation in a logical, rather than emotional, way.

Step 5: Step Outside Your Comfort Zone

1. **Apologize.** Sincerely apologize to your former spouse, your children, and yourself for how you have played a part in this event. Don't spend time playing the blame game. A sincere apology by you will help you heal more quickly. Accept, forgive, move on.

2. **Forge ahead.** Get comfortable with being uncomfortable. In other words, get back in the saddle. Make a concerted effort to meet new people, even if you initially have no interest in dating.

3. **Engage.** Find a support group. Use the group as a sounding board to heal, gain insights, and develop new skills (rather than as a venue to complain about the pain of the past), even if it initially makes you uncomfortable. A good support group can help you move past fear and gain greater clarity about positive next steps.

4. **Renew and refresh.** A divorce is an opportunity to have a paradigm shift. This is when you can give yourself a fresh start. Look for opportunities to make this a time of healing introspection. What do you need to do to renew and refresh yourself? Write a list and begin the quest today.

Commit to using these five steps to help you in times of difficulty and uncertainty, whether that is after the loss of a job, the death of a loved one, or in my case, divorce.

Be sure to work on your mental toughness training daily. As you begin achieving greater results from your training, the steps I have shared with you will feel more natural. By using the five steps, you will be able to face the future with greater confidence and enthusiasm.

Maintain Mental Toughness

Throughout these pages we have discussed mental toughness as a mind-set. A mentally tough mind-set is much like any other skill you have ever acquired; it must be worked on continuously. Mentally tough people don't let their skills slip. They routinely work (even subconsciously) on their mental toughness, whether through new challenges, reassessments, or in their own unique ways.

Whether it is learning to play the guitar, learning Spanish, or working on mind-set management, the skills must be consistently worked on. Developing a mentally tough mind-set requires continual work. Without work, the benefits will quickly wear off.

SURROUND YOURSELF WITH ENCOURAGEMENT

One easy way to stay on track and motivated to continue working on your mental toughness training is to surround yourself with encouragement. I already suggested keeping inspirational quotes on hand, but there are other things you can do to remind yourself to keep going. Here are several ideas that help keep people on track:

- Create a playlist that you can listen to when you're thinking about slacking off. The pieces you choose can range from music that moves you to podcasts that inspire.

- Pick up a biography of someone you greatly admire. Reading about how they overcame adversity can really light a fire in you.

- Watch a movie that focuses on mental toughness, such as *Rudy*, *Stand and Deliver*, or even *The Empire Strikes Back*!

- Talk to friends and family about their mental toughness. Ask them to describe how they overcame obstacles on the way to their goals. Knowing how they stayed mentally tough will help you stay mentally tough, too.

Always keep in mind that mental toughness isn't just for the marines, the business leaders, or the star athletes. Mental toughness can be achieved by anyone who works hard and hones their mental toughness skills. Former SEAL and *New York Times* bestselling author Brandon Webb points out that "There is a common [misconception] that to make it through SEAL training you have to be a super athlete. Not so. In its purely physical requirements, the course is designed for the average athletic male to be able to make it through." The same is true of mental toughness training. You have the skills; you just need to use them, practice them, and make them part of your everyday life.

To continue building mental toughness, you must always have something to strive for: a graduate degree, re-entering the workforce after raising children, completing your first marathon, or anything else that is worthy of your time and effort. By continually looking for opportunities to test your physical, emotional, and spiritual well-being, you dramatically increase the likelihood of living a fulfilled life. And by challenging yourself, you are more likely to develop a mental toughness mind-set that will help you in times of sudden misfortune. Creating a mentally tough mind-set will not always be easy, but it will always be worth it, because it will strengthen you as a person.

Along with using these quick methods of encouragement to stay on your mental toughness path, you'll need long-term strategies to take your mental toughness skills into the future. If you have followed the five steps in this book you have already grown in strength and confidence and can take this strength and confidence to the next level. How?

Serve first. Mentally tough people are not people pleasers; they take action and make decisions that serve the interests of others first. By leading in this way, mentally tough people gain respect and loyalty from others.

Create a specific vision. Mentally tough people can't serve others without having a specific vision for where they want to go. They develop this vision and effectively communicate it to others.

Respect others' time. By respecting boundaries, mentally tough people send a message that they value their own time and the time and sacrifices of others.

Prioritize well-being. Just as you have learned to prioritize your well-being as you are developing your mental toughness mind-set, mentally tough people set schedules that incorporate breaks and relaxation because they know they can't perform at their highest if they are tired mentally and physically.

Act with integrity. Mentally tough people know that they must inspire and respect others. Successful mentally tough people focus on building up others, not tearing them down.

Have relentless spirit. Mentally tough people show grit every day. They do everything they can to recover from setbacks and forge ahead with optimism.

Not surprisingly, each of these methods for long-term mental toughness is practiced by leaders in the military, the business world, politics, the world of sports, and in communities around the world, since successful leaders are inevitably mentally tough. With your mental toughness skills, you have leadership qualities in you, too.

Face Challenges Head-On

You may find that you've followed the five steps, developed a mental tough-ness mind-set, and practiced your mental toughness skills, both in the short and long term. But then you're side-swiped by an unforeseen setback: a business failure, a personal tragedy, a family emergency. How can you maintain and use your mental toughness under such adverse circumstances?

Although challenges can be difficult to face head-on, the quickest way to extinguish the angst created by any difficult challenge is to move fast. The reason is simple: the faster we address the difficult situation, the faster we can begin to work on making it better. Too often that is not what we do. Instead, we allow the challenge to fester within us, creating additional stress.

How can you maintain and use your mental toughness under an unusually adverse circumstance? By implementing the following steps as soon as you are faced with a difficult challenge. I am not saying it will be easy, but it will be worth the effort.

1. Take ownership of any part of the challenge that you may have created.
2. Commit to addressing the challenge as soon as practical.
3. Don't spend needless energy dwelling on why the challenge has arisen.
4. Engage the support of a mentor who can help you gain insights or possible solutions.
5. Get a good night's sleep and commit to addressing the situation early the next day when you're rested.
6. Call or meet with anyone who has been or will be affected by the challenge.
7. Identify and explain or ask for reasons—not excuses—as to why the challenge has occurred.
8. Apologize if warranted.
9. Offer or ask for possible solutions on how the situation can be improved.
10. Immediately implement the agreed-upon solutions.
11. Forgive yourself and others. Release the angst. Learn from the challenge.

Mentally tough people face challenges head-on in order to keep moving forward toward their goals and the best version of themselves.

Celebrate Others' Successes—and Yours!

Inspirational speaker Croix Sather talks about the importance of looking for opportunities to elevate others by celebrating their achievements. It is his belief that the more we honor and celebrate the achievements of others, the greater the likelihood that our own station in life will be elevated and improved.

Many people move through life tearing down those around them in an effort to make themselves appear bigger. Mentally tough people, on the other hand, routinely elevate others and celebrate their successes. They are not threatened by others' accomplishments; instead, they know that calling out others for their accomplishments benefits everyone. This can be done through a simple acknowledgment of a job well done at a company meeting or a short thank-you note to a teacher who went above and beyond the call of duty. Studies show that being praised for good work is higher on the job satisfaction list than money.

Today and every day, praise the accomplishments of the first five people you see. Think of something that you can say to them that will build them up. Tell a fellow parishioner that you appreciate their willingness to share their time, talent, and treasures with the congregation because it has had meaningful impact. Tell a co-worker how much you appreciate their hard work or honesty. Tell your spouse, child, or another family member how much you value all of the love and support they give you. Be as specific as possible so the person you are trying to elevate knows you are being authentic and that you genuinely care.

If there is one lesson I hope you take away from this book, it is that mental toughness can give you the life you want. Your mentally tough mind-set will give you the self-confidence you need to change the way you look at the world around you. Challenges that you once viewed with fear will be transformed into opportunities. And these opportunities will enable you to pursue your biggest goals and wildest dreams in life. I wish you the greatest success imaginable.

RESOURCES

Afremow, Jim. *The Champion's Mind: How Great Athletes Think, Train, and Thrive.* Rodale Books, 2014.

Brown, Brené. *Braving the Wilderness: The Quest for True Belonging and the Courage to Stand Alone.* Random House, 2017.

Brown, Brené. *Daring Greatly: How the Courage to Be Vulnerable Transforms the Way We Live, Love, Parent, and Lead.* Avery, 2012.

Colebrooke, Lawrence. *Special Operations Mental Toughness: The Invincible Mindset of Delta Force Operators, Navy SEALs, Army Rangers & Other Elite Warriors!* Self-published, 2015.

Duckworth, Angela. *Grit: The Power of Passion and Perseverance.* Scribner, 2016.

Gonzalez, D.C. *The Art of Mental Training: A Guide to Performance Excellence.* Self-published, 2013.

Lambertsen, Chris. *Navy SEAL Mental Toughness: A Guide to Developing an Unbeatable Mind.* Self-published, 2016.

McCormack, Mark H. *What They Don't Teach You at Harvard Business School: Notes from a Street-Smart Executive.* Bantam, 1986.

Selk, Jason. *10-Minute Toughness: The Mental Training Program for Winning Before the Game Begins.* McGraw-Hill Education, 2008.

Thoreau, Henry D. *Walden, Or, Life in the Woods.* Dent, 1908.

REFERENCES

Bourgeois, Trudy. "The Greatest Gift — To: You and I, From: Nelson Mandela." Last modified February, 18, 2014. Accessed June 20, 2018. https://www.huffingtonpost.com/trudy-bourgeois/the-greatest-gift_b_4469297.html.

Browne, Ian. "Roberts' Steal Set Amazing 2004 Playoff Run in Motion." October 17, 2014. Accessed June 20, 2018. https://www.mlb.com/news/dave-roberts-steal-set-amazing-2004-red-sox-playoff-run-in-motion/c-98844328.

Canfield, Jack. "Visualization Techniques to Affirm Your Desired Outcomes: A Step-by-Step Guide." Accessed June 20, 2018. http://jackcanfield.com/blog/visualize-and-affirm-your-desired-outcomes-a-step-by-step-guide/.

Chu, Charles. "Bulletproof Mind: 6 Secrets of Mental Toughness from the Navy SEALs." November 25, 2016. Accessed June 20, 2018. http://observer.com/2016/11/bulletproof-mind-6-secrets-of-mental-toughness-from-the-navy-seals/.

Duckworth, Angela. "Quiz: How Much Grit Do You Have?" Last modified February 29, 2016. Accessed June 20, 2018. https://www.nytimes.com/interactive/2016/03/01/us/01grit-quiz.html.

Jabr, Ferris. "Why Your Brain Needs More Downtime." October 15, 2013. Accessed June 20, 2018. https://www.scientificamerican.com/article/mental-downtime/.

Hebrews 11:1 (King James Version).

Loder, Vanessa. "The Power of Vision – What Entrepreneurs Can Learn from Olympic Athletes." July 23, 2014. Accessed June 20, 2018. https://www.forbes.com/sites/vanessaloder/2014/07/23/the-power-of-vision-what-entrepreneurs-can-learn-from-olympic-athletes/#323db0c66e74.

Samson, Andrea C. and James J. Gross. "Humour as Emotion Regulation: The Differential Consequences of Negative Versus Positive Humour." Cognition & Emotion 26, no. 2 (2012): 375–84. doi:10.1080/02699931.2011.585069.

Savara, Sid. "Why 3% of Harvard MBAs Make Ten Times as Much as the Other 97% Combined." Accessed June 20, 2018. https://sidsavara.com/why-3-of-harvard-mbas-make-ten-times-as-much-as-the-other-97-combined/.

Zimmerman, Eilene. "Survey Shows Visualizing Success Works." January 27, 2016. Accessed June 20, 2018. https://www.forbes.com/sites/eilenezimmerman/2016/01/27/survey-shows-visualizing-success-works/#2f5a49aa760b.

INDEX

A

Accountability, 17
Achor, Shawn, 56
Active engagement, 54
Active forgiveness, 13
Adaptability, 70
Alpha awareness, 62
Anxiety. *See* Fear
Attributes, of mental toughness, 5–9
Authentic self, 36–37

B

Boyatzis, Richard, 70
Brown, Brené, 69
Brown, Les, 54

C

Canfield, Jack, 56
Carrey, Jim, 28
Challenges, 73, 89–90
Change, adapting to, 60–61, 69
Comfort zones, 11, 68–69
    benefits of discomfort, 71–73
    benefits of moving out of, 69–71
    divorce example, 86
Compromising, 62
Confidence, 73
Contentment, 37
Control, 21–25, 63–64
Coolidge, Calvin, 74
Core beliefs, 29–35

D

Disney, Walt, 59
Distractions, 65
Doss, Desmond T., 60–61

E

Emotional distractions, 48–50.
    See also Positive thinking
Encouragement, 87
Excuses, 17–20

F

Failure, 14, 62, 68–69
Fear, 4, 9, 37, 72, 74–76
Flexibility, 10–11, 65
    in changing circumstances, 60–61
    divorce example, 85
    improving, 62
    recovering from challenges and
        setbacks, 59–60, 63–64, 89–90
Forgiveness, 13, 25

G

Gates, Bill, 59
Goal-setting
    and core beliefs, 29–35
    and fear, 74–76
    and goal achievement, 40–41, 43
    SMART method, 41–42
    visualization, 27–29
Gratitude, 52, 53–54

H

Happiness, 56
Humor, 61

I

Intentions, 13

J

Jabr, Ferris, 77

K

Keller, Helen, 69
Kittredge, Mike, 2–3

L

Letting go, 10, 12–13
    of bad habits, 24
    and control, 21–25
    divorce example, 82–83
    finding a mantra, 14–16
Lincoln, Abraham, 74

M

Managing the minute, 21
Mandela, Nelson, 13
Mantras, 14–16, 60
Mental flexibility. *See* Flexibility
Mental toughness
    benefits of, 3–4
    definition of, 1–2
    divorce example, 81–86
    maintaining, 87–90
    program overview, 10–11
    qualities of, 2–3

Mental toughness wheel, 5–9
Mindfulness, 13
Mind-set training, 4, 15, 27, 87–89
Mission statements, 10, 28–29, 43–45
    divorce example, 83–84
Moral compass, 35
Motivation, 38–39, 52
Moving on, 64
Musk, Elon, 10

N

Navy SEALs, 67–68
Negative emotions, 48–50, 54.
        See also Positive thinking
Neutral positioning statements
    (NPS), 60

O

Optimism, 53–55

P

Pattern identification, 13
Penney, James Cash, 40
Plumb, Charlie, 50–52
Positive thinking, 10, 50–52, 55–56.
        See also Optimism
    divorce example, 84–85
Praising others, 90–91
Pre-playing, 27, 64
Procrastination, 75
Productivity, 70–71

R

Reasons, vs. excuses, 17–20
Recovery stage, 63–64

Refresh, renew,
     revive, 76–78
Resilience, 3, 53, 59, 77
Rewards, 62
Roberts, Dave, 47–48

S

Sather, Croix, 90
Self-acceptance, 13
Self-care, 76–78
Self-love, 37
Serenity Prayer, 21
Setbacks, 59
Solitude, 55
"So What Method," 33–34
Success, 35–38, 56, 90–91

T

Taking charge, 17, 24
     divorce example, 82–83
Thoreau, Henry David, 24

V

Victimhood, 63
Visualization, 27–29, 55–56
Vonn, Lindsey, 27–28

W

Webb, Anthony Jerome "Spud," 3
Webb, Brandon, 88
Well-being, 24, 49–50, 77
"What if" self-talk, 75

ACKNOWLEDGMENTS

In 2018, my big goal was to write my first book. I had every intention to self-publish.

I never considered reaching out to a publisher with the hope they might want me as their author. You can imagine my surprise and thankfulness when Meg Ilasco from Callisto Media called me and offered me a book deal. I am confident this is evidence that the universe will help you honor your intention when your focus is to help improve the lives of others.

The team at Callisto Media has been amazing to work with. They have kept me on track and never stopped believing that I was the right person to write this book.

I owe special thanks to so many people that helped make this project possible, including Kathy Dunn of Main Street Writers.

To my fellow members of *The Brotherhood of the Queen's Ear,* including Duane Cashin, Dave Hasenbalg, Marty McMahon, Eddie Gautier, and John Jahrstorfer, thank you for listening and supporting me on this journey. I can't wait to give you a copy!

Special shout-out to the many inspirational guides I have been blessed with, including: Diane Stewart, Anne Marie Demonte, John Cook, Keith Albright, Marcy McDonald, Liz Fry, Greg Kohut, Jim Bayles, Loretta Cox, Croix Sather, Jake McLay, Tim Preiser, Mike and Lisa Kittredge, Liberty Forrest, Lorretta and Geoff Cox, My Hut Brothers and Sisters, Phil and Martha Swasey, Kurt Grosvenor, Frank Salomon Sr., Kelly Witt, Eileen Moran, Jen Sweet, Sarah Morris, Harlan Reycroft, Nick Salvatore, Irving Schwartzbach, Sim Kaye, Dorothy Graham, and everyone in District 53 Toastmasters.

Lastly, and most importantly, there is no one more responsible in supporting my dreams than my family. Special thanks to my sister Laurie Comstock Ferguson and my brothers Clint and Bryan Comstock for always being there for me when I needed them most.

To my Mom and Dad, although you are no longer with us, your children recognize that we won the lottery of life having you as our parents. Thank you for giving each one of us wings and then, more importantly, flying lessons.

To my children, Kendall, Haley, and Jordin, thank you for always believing in me. You are my greatest treasures. It is so important to me that I got to write this book as a gift to you. My hope is that as you continue to grow into adulthood and face your own challenges, perhaps something you read within these pages will comfort you and give you direction. Always remember the motto of Team Turtle when facing any challenge: The first thing your brain needs to say is, "I CAN DO IT!"

Finally, to Mary Jean Roy, my wife of 22 years. Thank you for being a gift in my life on so many levels.

ABOUT THE AUTHOR

DOUGLAS CLYDESDALE COMSTOCK is an entrepreneur and award-winning speaker on the topic of mental toughness, leadership, and high performance.

Doug inspires his audiences by relating motivational lessons from his experiences as a former Alaska "Deadliest Catch" commercial fisherman, two-time finisher of the Hawaii Ironman Triathlon, and 3rd Degree Black Belt team member on the US Intersport Karate team to Russia. At age 60, Doug swam for 13 hours and 20 minutes, covering 19 miles across the English Channel.

He is the founder of GettingToGoal.com speaking and coaching services. He is also the founding partner of and currently directs the largest on-site AED maintenance company in North America, AEDserviceAmerica.com.

His clients include Aetna, Hartford Insurance, McDonalds, NBC, Harvard Business School, Providence College, Webster Bank, New England Patriots, and Yankee Candle, as well as celebrity clients Meryl Streep, Robert Redford, Fleetwood Mac, and hundreds more.

For further information, call 860-970-3250 or email dc@GettingToGoal.com.

)

CPSIA information can be obtained
at www.ICGtesting.com
Printed in the USA
LVHW07s1435290918
591425LV00005B/2/P